Being British

This book is dedicated to Maureen Hughes who lost her brave battle against ovarian cancer in 2014, halfway through writing this book. Her son, Kieran, continued her work.

Being British

Maureen Hughes and Kieran Hughes

PEN & SWORD HISTORY

First published in Great Britain in 2017 by
Pen & Sword History
an imprint of
Pen & Sword Books Ltd
47 Church Street
Barnsley
South Yorkshire
S70 2AS

ISBN 978 1 84468 075 7

Typeset in Ehrhardt by
Mac Style Ltd, Bridlington, East Yorkshire
Printed and bound in Malta by Gutenberg Press Ltd.

Pen & Sword Books Ltd incorporates the imprints of Pen & Sword
Archaeology, Atlas, Aviation, Battleground, Discovery, Family
History, History, Maritime, Military, Naval, Politics, Railways, Select,
Transport, True Crime, Fiction, Frontline Books, Leo Cooper,
Praetorian Press, Seaforth Publishing and Wharncliffe.

For a complete list of Pen & Sword titles please contact
PEN & SWORD BOOKS LIMITED
47 Church Street, Barnsley, South Yorkshire, S70 2AS, England
E-mail: enquiries@pen-and-sword.co.uk
Website: www.pen-and-sword.co.uk

Contents

Introduction

A number of recent surveys of what makes Britain great, read before writing this book, seem to feature some recurring themes and topics. They nearly always include the countryside, roast dinners, fish and chips, cream teas, the Queen, Stonehenge, Cornish pasties, James Bond, historic buildings and Shakespeare. There is so much in Britain worthy of celebration but unfortunately it has only been possible to pick a few examples. Apologies if your favourite place, food, hobby or attribute is not featured. Hopefully, this book will remind you how great it is to be British and for those wanting to settle here, provide a little something about our customs, history and idiosyncrasies.

Acknowledgements

Many people have helped the both of us to put this book together over the years, including the following family, friends and organisations: David Benson (my dad), Bethan Hughes, Gail Hughes, Geraint Hughes, Hugh Mothersole, Hilary Elston, Cadbury's, Phil Seaman, Bridget Hughes and Kirstin Pettet. Apologies if I have missed out anyone else who helped along the way.

Kieran Hughes
May 2017

Chapter 1

The Geography of Britain and Its Counties

Q. What is the Difference Between the United Kingdom and Great Britain? Worryingly this seems to be a question that many British people fail to answer correctly. The answer is quite complicated and transcends both politics and geography.

1. The United Kingdom comprises England, Scotland, Wales and Northern Ireland.
2. Great Britain comprises only England, Scotland and Wales.
3. Britain comprises England and Wales.
4. The British Isles comprise England, Scotland and Wales, several islands, of which Great Britain is the largest, and the Republic of Ireland as well.

England, formerly known as *Engla Land,* covers an area of over 50,000 sq. miles and its capital is London. It is the birthplace of the English language and this is spoken by the majority of the English population.

Scotland covers an area of over 30,000 sq. miles and its capital is Edinburgh. Although it does have its own language, the majority of Scottish people choose to speak English in everyday life, albeit it with an accent that, although very attractive to the ear, some may find difficult to understand.

Wales covers an area of over 8,000 sq. miles and its capital is Cardiff. Wales, like Scotland, does have its own language but, unlike the Scots, many of the Welsh people are bilingual and conduct their everyday business in their own language, particularly in the north of the country.

Northern Ireland, commonly referred to as Ulster, was once part of Catholic Ireland until Elizabeth I (1558–1603) suppressed three rebellions in the area and invited Scots Presbyterians to settle in the region after confiscating Catholic lands. Anglican Englishmen settled in Ulster in the seventeenth century after further rebellions, thus reinforcing a Catholic–Protestant divide. Protestant settlements flourished in Ulster on the back of preferential political treatment. Northern Ireland became a political entity when the six counties accepted the Home Rule Bill of 1920, with a semi-autonomous parliament but indirect rule from the Cabinet. Today, there is still a Catholic majority in Southern Ireland and a Protestant majority in Northern Ireland.

A Walk Around the Counties of Great Britain

Great Britain is divided into the countries of England, Scotland and Wales and then subdivided into counties. The residents of each of these counties are territorially very proud of their cultural heritage and geographical presence, so much so that to some extent when one crosses the county border it is sometimes akin to crossing a *country* border! Most British people are fiercely proud of where they were born; and it is just that – where they were born and not where they necessarily grew up or have lived for most of their lives. There is no definitive number of counties as borders change – generally for administrative reasons. For the purpose of this book, though at the risk of offending some, a number of counties have been selected for closer examination; the only reason for omitting others is lack of space.

England

County	County Town	Famous For
Bedfordshire	Bedford	If you enjoy beautiful gardens, then here you will find The Swiss Garden, originally laid out in the early nineteenth century.
Berkshire	Reading	Also known as 'Royal Berkshire', it is the home of the magnificent Windsor Castle. Here you will also find the world-famous Eton School where many English monarchs and heads of government have been educated. Also, the village of Thatcham, which claims to be the oldest inhabited village in England. Or alternatively spend a day at the races at Royal Ascot.
Buckinghamshire	Aylesbury	In Buckinghamshire you will find Chequers, the country residence of the Prime Minister in office; the house is not open to the public.
Cambridgeshire	Cambridge	The home of the world-famous and historic seat of learning, the University of Cambridge, with its colleges dating as far back as 1284. In this county one can take a leisurely punt on the river or visit Ely Cathedral, also known as 'The Ship of the Fens'.
Cheshire	Chester	The history of this north-western town dates back over 4,000 years. Here you might be lucky and catch the Chester Mystery Plays, which are played out every four years.
Cornwall	Truro	Renowned for its tales and legends of King Arthur, as well as its delicious Cornish pasties, Cornwall has an abundance of attractions for its visitors including secluded sandy beaches and the popular surfers' beaches.
County Durham	Durham	Known as one of the 'Beautiful Counties', it is the home of Durham University, Auckland Castle, which is the official residence of the Bishop of Durham, and Durham Cathedral.
Derbyshire	Matlock	Derbyshire nestles in the heart of England and is dominated by the Peak District, England's first National Park. Several stately homes can also be found in the county.

County	County Town	Famous For
Devon	Exeter	The birthplace of Agatha Christie and Sir Francis Drake, Devon has many beautiful beaches, not to mention those wonderful cream teas of scones and clotted cream – not the place to visit if you are on a diet!
Kent	Maidstone	Kent is known as the Garden of England. Canterbury Cathedral has been the seat of the Archbishop of Canterbury since the sixth century. Kent is nestled between London and the Strait of Dover. The county forms the south-eastern corner of England and is a mere 21 miles from France.
Shropshire	Shrewsbury	The home town of Maureen, Shrewsbury is a market town at the heart of rural Shropshire (once referred to as Salop). This medieval market town is home to 70,000 people and has 600 listed buildings including the Castle and Shrewsbury Abbey, which are at the heart of the town. Charles Darwin was perhaps the town's most famous resident.
Surrey	Guildford	The county is known for its abundance of trees and leafy lanes; so beautiful are they that the branches of a tree lining one side of a lane frequently reach over to join the branches of a tree on the other side of the lane, and so form an archway.
Yorkshire	York	Yorkshire is the largest of the English counties and is divided into three different regions, called Ridings – East, North and West Riding. Bordering the North Sea, it has numerous pretty fishing villages and is famed for its wild and desolate North York Moors. The historic county town of York, dominated by York Minster, is one of the most visited towns in England. Meanwhile, yorkshire-england.co.uk highlights an important change in 1974, stating that 'the three ridings of Yorkshire were abolished and York, which had been a county in its own right, independent of the ridings, was incorporated into the new county called North Yorkshire'.

Chapter 2

British Landmarks

People often ask where they should visit when holidaying in Great Britain, be they British or from foreign shores. Well, the initial answer has got to be: 'How long have you got?' You would need a year-long holiday, and still you wouldn't see all that Britain has to offer. It is a country rich in history, sparkling with beauty and calm in the serenity of a green and wonderful land. One of the major problems in compiling this book was deciding what to include and what to omit. This chapter alone could fill several books, but space precludes that so we have attempted to whet your appetite and hopefully encourage you to experience more than the tip of the iceberg.

A Selection of Interesting Places to Visit

Sight	Description
Big Ben	This landmark is often taken in as a part of a tour of London, and that's fine – just don't come to London without seeing Big Ben because then your visit will be incomplete. It doesn't exist just to tell you the time, it's to tell you that you have arrived in one of the greatest cities in the world! Big Ben is actually the name of the bell and not the clock tower, as most people assume. Completed in 1859, the Great Clock started on 31 May and the Great Bell's strikes were heard for the first time on 11 July.
Blackpool Tower	Originally opening to the public on 14 May 1894, Blackpool Tower, which was inspired by the Eiffel Tower in Paris, dominates the Lancashire seaside town of Blackpool, its very name synonymous with ballroom dancing throughout the world. It stands at 518ft high.
Buckingham Palace	Buckingham Palace. (*Photo: Kieran Hughes*) This is the official residence of the Queen and the Duke of Edinburgh and their personal staff. It has a total of 92 offices, 240 bedrooms and 19 state rooms, amongst other rooms. It was originally a much smaller property, built as a private townhouse for the Duke of Buckingham in 1703. King George II purchased the attractive little townhouse and it was extended and remodelled as a palace over the next seventy years and three monarchs, at a huge and spiralling cost. The new palace was first occupied by Queen Victoria when she came to the throne in 1837. It was bombed on a number of occasions during the Second World War, much to the relief of the Queen Consort, Elizabeth, who felt she could better sympathise with the people of the West End as a result of this.

Sight	Description
Hadrian's Wall	Hadrian's Wall is one of the most popular attractions in the North of England. It was a defensive fortification of the Roman Empire, situated on the border of the empire and running from coast to coast. It was punctuated with castles, garrisons, barracks, forts, cavalry and gates to keep out the savage Scots. Large sections of the wall still remain intact. Hadrian's Wall is named after Emperor Hadrian who ordered its construction. The 73-mile structure was started in about AD 122, and took 15,000 men a total of 6 years to complete. It was a major border post for almost 300 years.
Hampton Court	 Hampton Court. (*Photo: Kieran Hughes*) Hampton Court has not been inhabited by the British royal family since the eighteenth century. Hampton Court and St James's Palace are the only two remaining palaces of Henry VIII and for that reason alone are worthy of visiting. Apart from the buildings and rooms, younger visitors will enjoy trying to find their way out of the historic maze.
Highlands of Scotland	The Highlands of Scotland offer spectacular scenery, with mountains, lochs and glens. At Loch Lomond you may see the elusive Loch Ness Monster, proving once and for all that it really does exist! The wildlife is magnificent and the men wear kilts and play bagpipes – granted not all of them, but enough to warrant a visit!
Houses of Parliament	Apart from those politically aware or at the very least interested, this is another sight often taken in from the top of a tour bus. This is essential in making a trip to London complete!
Oxford	Oxford is the home of that great seat of learning – Oxford University – but is also a great city to visit in its own right.

Sight	Description
St Paul's Cathedral	One of the many churches in London, it was chosen by Prince Charles and Lady Diana Spencer for their wedding in 1981. Climb the 259 steps up to the dome and there you will find the Whispering Gallery, which runs around the interior of the dome. It gets its name from a quirk in its construction, which makes a whisper against its walls audible on the opposite side – children love it!
Snowdonia	The National Park of Snowdonia is stunning with its snow-capped mountains, rolling hills and the Swallow Falls of Betws-y-Coed. It is tranquil, serene and calming for those usually embroiled in the rat race of twenty-first-century living. Visitors can either walk up Mount Snowdon or take the mountain railroad. There are beautiful walks for the energetic and quaint tea stops for those who just like to sit and watch the world roll by as they listen to the beautiful Welsh language native to the area. Drive on through Betws-y-Coed towards the coast and you will be enthralled by the lovely little seaside towns that time forgot, such as Llanddudno, Beaumaris and Menai Bridge, which overlooks the stunning Menai Strait. Escape the hustle and bustle of everyday living and relax in Snowdonia.
Stonehenge	One of Britain's oldest structures is the prehistoric monument of standing stones in Wiltshire known as Stonehenge. A World Heritage Site since 1986, archaeologists believe it was constructed somewhere between 3000 to 2000 BC. At the time of going to press, The Association of Leading Visitor Attractions reported the last annual visitor numbers to Stonehenge were 1,366,758.
Stratford-upon-Avon	This small Warwickshire market town situated on the River Avon attracts more than 5 million tourists a year as it was the birthplace of William Shakespeare. It is also home to The Royal Shakespeare Company. Discover-stratford.com promotes tours to buildings directly associated with the Bard (Shakespeare). It states, 'The five houses offer a multi-layered experience for visitors unlike any other, giving people from all over the world the opportunity to learn about the life of the world's greatest playwright, discover his work and experience a real sense of the times that influenced him in Stratford-upon-Avon.'

Sight	Description
Tower of London	Work on the Tower of London began in the early 1080s and it was to become a fortress to keep people out or keep people in! Throughout its long history it has been a royal palace, a prison, a place of execution, a royal arsenal and a treasury, which today stores the Crown Jewels. The walls of the Tower have witnessed some dark deeds and this famous attraction is said to be haunted too, so if you are partial to the odd ghost, this is the place to visit! Yeoman Warders – nicknamed Beefeaters – conduct very popular tours of the Tower enthralling visitors with tales of imprisonment, execution and torture. And of course you must try to spot one of the six resident ravens, for it is said that the Tower and the Kingdom will fall if they ever leave the fortress.
Windsor Castle	Curfew Tower, Windsor Castle. (*Photo: Kieran Hughes*) This is the largest inhabited castle in the world. It is home or work to 500 people and remains the usual weekend retreat for Queen Elizabeth II. During the Second World War it was also a refuge from the intense London bombing around Buckingham Palace. Its construction began in the eleventh century and it survived the Civil War and Interregnum, as well as a major fire in 1992. The castle is open most of the year for tourists. Private royal apartments are located at the rear of the castle, including a private pool and luxurious royal bedrooms. St George's Chapel is situated inside the castle grounds, and remains a favourite for royal christenings and services.

Sight	Description
York	York Minster. (*Photo: Hugh Mothersole*) The beautiful and historic city of York is the home town of one of the co-authors and so we feel that a tour of Great Britain would be incomplete unless York was on the itinerary! With its Roman, Viking and medieval heritage, York is splendid in the extreme. It is a city surrounded by medieval bar walls and dominated by the floodlit York Minster, the largest Gothic cathedral in northern Europe. Visiting York is like stepping back in time, with so much to see and do. There is the world-famous Jorvik Viking Centre, where visitors can experience a journey along Viking Age streets as they would have been more than a thousand years ago. And it's not pretend, it's all real and exciting! A visit to the Shambles, with its overhanging buildings that date back to the late fourteenth and fifteenth centuries, is an absolute must too.

For spectacular scenery the Highlands of Scotland provides some of the best, covering a huge expanse of land full of mountains, lochs and glens. The heritage of this area includes visiting Culloden, taking the ferry to the Isle of Skye or just viewing one of the many castles such as Eilean Donan. There is also the wildlife which includes ptarmigan, red grouse, ospreys, mountain hares, golden eagles, otters, red deer and pine martins. For the more adventurous, there is Aviemore in the heart of the Cairngorms National Park or Fort William, the outdoor capital of the UK that sits beneath Ben Nevis, both with superb mountain biking, hill climbing, skiing and watersports all available. For children, a trip to Loch Ness to see the Loch Ness Monster is a must! Alternatively there is the Kincraig Wildlife Park or the Landmark

Activity Centre at Carrbridge which are ideal for family fun. Many signposts are written in both English and Gaelic, the Scottish language. Shinty is the local sport, which to an outsider is the equivalent of hockey without rules.

The islands include the Inner and Outer Hebrides as well as the Orkney and Shetland islands. Orkney's ancient heritage dates back 6 millennia and Skara Brae is one of the finest preserved Stone-Age site in Europe and forms part of the islands' World Heritage Site. The best way of seeing Orkney is by touring the island which allows you to see the full effect of Scapa Flow and the Churchill Barriers. Island hopping is also popular and there is nothing better than enjoying the local food and drink of an evening or visiting the Highland Park Distillery in Kirkwall. For those going to Shetland, the annual Up Helly Aa and the Shetland Folk Festival are well worth catching. Once seen, never forgotten.

There are so many visitor attractions in the UK but which are the most popular? The Association of Leading Visitor Attractions (ALVA) (Patron, HRH the Duke of York), which represents the views of Britain's main visitor attractions to government, industry and the public, publishes an annual league table of the most visited attractions.

Visits Made in 2015 to Visitor Attractions that have Membership of ALVA

Rank	Site	Total Visits
1.	British Museum	6,820,686
2.	The National Gallery	5,908,254
3.	Natural History Museum (South Kensington)	5,284,023
4.	Southbank Centre	5,102,883
5.	Tate Modern	4,712,581
6.	Victoria & Albert Museum (South Kensington)	3,432,325
7.	Science Museum	3,356,212
8.	Somerset House	3,235,104
9.	Tower of London	2,785,249
10.	National Portrait Gallery	2,145,486
11.	Library of Birmingham	1,828,999
12.	Chester Zoo	1,694,185
13.	Old Royal Naval College, Greenwich	1,676,055
14.	Westminster Abbey	1,664,850
15.	Royal Botanic Gardens, Kew	1,622,821
16.	St Paul's Cathedral	1,609,325
17.	British Library	1,579,270
18.	Edinburgh Castle	1,568,508
19.	National Museum of Scotland	1,567,310
20.	Scottish National Gallery	1,377,710
21.	Stonehenge	1,366,758
22.	National Maritime Museum	1,357,663
23.	Tate Britain	1,284,519
24.	ZSL London Zoo	1,265,911
25.	Kelvingrove Art Gallery and Museum	1,261,552
26.	Roman Baths and Pump Room	1,176,527

Rank	Site	Total Visits
27.	Riverside Museum	1,131,814
28.	IWM, London	1,104,670
29.	The Royal Academy of Arts	1,096,608
30.	RHS Garden Wisley	1,087,927
31.	National Museum of the Royal Navy	1,015,415
32.	The Royal Shakespeare Theatre and Swan Theatre	1,002,040
33.	Eden Project	960,029
34.	Canterbury Cathedral	957,355
35.	Birmingham Museum & Art Gallery	936,839
36.	Houses of Parliament	928,855
37.	Royal Botanic Gardens Edinburgh	889,420
38.	Museum of London	872,978
39.	Horniman Museum and Gardens	866,188
40.	Giant's Causeway	851,314
41.	Ashmolean Museum	847,716
42.	Tower Bridge Exhibition	786,603
43.	Royal Observatory, Greenwich	778,941
44.	National Football Museum	776,000
45.	Shakespeare Birthplace Trust	771,700
46.	Blenheim Palace, Oxfordshire	763,045
47.	Museum of Liverpool	747,263
48.	ZSL Whipsnade Zoo	736,900
49.	National Railway Museum	733,618
50.	Museum of Science and Industry	697,290
51.	Merseyside Maritime Museum	662,494
52.	World Museum	658,898

Rank	Site	Total Visits
53.	Oxford University Museum of Natural History	640,092
54.	Edinburgh Zoo	633,351
55.	Tate Liverpool	626,410
56.	Chatsworth House and Garden	622,191
57.	*Titanic* Belfast	621,521
58.	Bodleian Library	611,090
59.	National War Museum, Edinburgh	601,074
60.	Hampton Court Palace	598,851
61.	Gallery of Modern Art	589,791
62.	Leeds Castle	564,483
63.	Churchill War Rooms	499,078
64.	Woburn Safari Park	489,751
65.	International Slavery Museum	460,161
66.	Stirling Castle	458,932
67.	V&A Museum of Childhood	449,787
68.	National Media Museum	442,314
69.	Stourhead	418,207
70.	The Fitzwilliam Museum	417,781
71.	Pitt Rivers Museum	415,766
72.	Cliveden	391,827
73.	Attingham Park	391,470
74.	Waddesdon	389,992
75.	Kensington Palace	383,286
76.	Belton House	382,124
77.	RHS Garden Harlow Carr	377,014
78.	Fountains Abbey and Studley Royal	371,012
79.	People's Palace	362,795
80.	The Royal Air Force Museum, London	356,404

Rank	Site	Total Visits
81.	The Royal Air Force Museum, Cosford	354,650
82.	Larrybane	353,549
83.	Urquhart Castle	348,691
84.	Shakespeare's Globe	348,678
85.	Polesden Lacey	338,865
86.	*Mary Rose* Museum	337,716
87.	Beaulieu	335,065
88	Anglesey Abbey	334,448
89.	Dover Castle	331,480
90.	Nymans Garden	319,023
91.	The Scottish National Portrait Gallery	312,877
92.	Calke Abbey	309,703
93.	St Michael's Mount	309,327
94.	HMS *Belfast*	299,858
95.	Mottisfont	294,654
96.	IWM, North	292,448
97.	Kingston Lacy	292,402
98.	IWM, Duxford	278,000
99.	Dunham Massey	277,324
100.	Museum of London Docklands	270,969

Figures reproduced by kind permission of alva.com.

Chapter 3

Food

Traditional British Food

British cuisine – and yes we do have the right to use the word 'cuisine' – is of the finest standard. Remember, we once had an empire and so have had an international input into our dishes. Many mock British food as being either bland or stodgy, but then the envious always ridicule! Our traditional dishes are an eclectic collection of culinary masterpieces and often a geographical and historical representation of the British way of life too, with supporting and fascinating stories regarding their evolvement and development, stories that can be told at dinner parties. Whether you are one who loves or one who despises British cuisine is somewhat irrelevant, for there is still an impressive array of foods traditional both in terms of region and history. For visitors from abroad it can at times be a little confusing for much depends upon regional differences, preferences and traditions. Some of the unusually named traditional foods you might come across in Britain are bara brith, a tasty welsh bread (*bara*), black pudding, bubble and squeak, Cornish pasties, Eccles cake, Irish stew, jellied eels and Lancashire hotpot.

Let's start with the timings of, and the names given to, meal times. This is where the great British divide comes into play. In the North, meal times are called 'Breakfast', 'Dinner' and 'Tea', whereas in the South meal times are called 'Breakfast', 'Lunch' and 'Dinner'. The names have nothing to do with the meal that is being eaten either, just the timings of the three meals! So a man can come home in the North to have his main meal of the day and it will still be called tea. Southerners can seemingly be a little snobbish about this and insist that a meal eaten in the evening is dinner. Let us now take a look at traditional British fayre.

Fish and Chips

Now most would insist that this is the most famous of traditional English fayre, and many would argue the most delicious too! Initially there tended to be a North–South divide with this food, with chips being a cheap and staple food of the North, whilst fried fish was introduced into London's East End. (The great Charles Dickens referred to a 'fried fish warehouse' in his novel *Oliver Twist*.) Then some enterprising individual decided to marry the two, and so the national dish of 'Fish 'n Chips', as we know it today, was born. The Northerners laid claim to the opening of the first fish and chip shop in Mossely, near Oldham, Lancashire, in about 1863. And how do we know that? The owner of the said shop had the foresight to put a sign in his window declaring: 'This is the first fish and chip shop in the world'. During the Second World War the government tried to make sure fish and chips were not rationed like other foods, in order to help boost morale back home. The interesting fact is, though, that not only is it a traditional food but it is also surrounded by traditional ways of consuming it, ways though that have sadly being confined to memory as we become more and more health and hygiene conscious.

Whilst this dish is eaten throughout the British Isles it is thought by many, including the British themselves, to be a 'Northern dish'. And as a Northern lass descended from a line of East Coast fishermen, Maureen didn't mind that at all and was quite proud of it. Visit any seaside town (especially in the North) and you will find numerous fish and chip shops. In the 1950s, fish and chips were traditionally eaten out of newspaper whilst walking down the street (or better still along a British seaside promenade – traditionally called a 'front'), and of course using only the fingers. Now this behaviour would be deemed as 'common' and dangerously unhygienic, but then it was oh so delicious and oh so very, very British! Somehow the food tasted better this way and no one cared a jot that their fingers were covered in newspaper print, print that they then calmly transferred to the food before eating it. Can you imagine that happening now? Everyone would be convinced that their days were numbered once they had eaten but half a dozen chips. Is this a case of health and safety gone mad or a case of common sense prevailing at last?

In Yorkshire there was an entire language surrounding this food too, where a chip shop could be found on virtually every street corner in the 1950s and 1960s and at this time everyone had their favourite 'chippie' too. Maureen distinctly remembers her parents making her cycle 2 miles there and back every Friday to their personal favourite chippie, despite actually living next door to one, and it was there that the chippie-specific language came into play. In fact, it wasn't until she moved south and tried to order fish and chips in a Southern chippie that she realised this was regional speak and could not be understood by the foreign Southerners! It went like this:

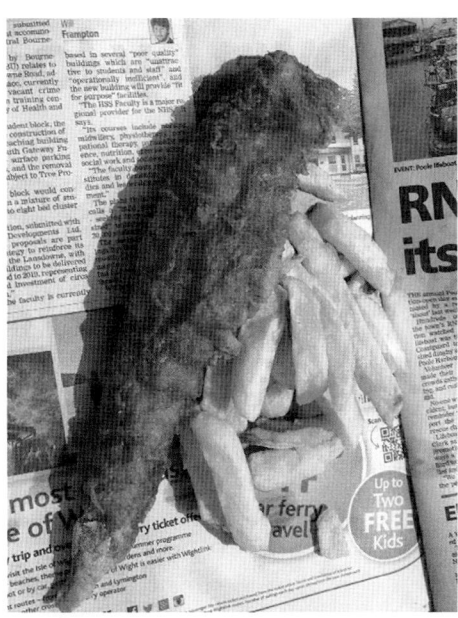

The once life-threatening (and now banned) fish and chips served in newspaper. (*Photo: Kieran Hughes*)

- 'One of each' meaning 'One fish and a bag of chips'.
- 'Two of each and a bag of chips' meaning 'Two fish, two bags of chips plus an extra bag of chips'.
- 'Bag of scraps' meaning 'Bag of the scraps of batter that had fallen off the fish when it was frying'. This was usually free and so a favourite with children!

In other parts of the British Isles there were regional variations; in 'Geordie Land', for example, a fish was referred to as 'a paper' and scraps were 'scruncheons'. All of this proves that whilst Britain has traditions, different regions of the country have their own variations on these too. Confusing for the British? Try being a visitor!

Bangers and Mash

Some think that bangers and mash originated during the Second World War, but its birth was in fact much earlier on in the twentieth century. The term 'bangers' was given to sausages because the cheaper varieties (especially during periods of rationing during the two world wars) were higher in fat content than in meat and so, when cooked on a high heat, had a tendency to 'explode'. Potatoes have, of course, always been a staple food in Britain and so mash was commonly consumed by the poor. However, in recent years it has became a rather trendy dish and now appears on many a restaurant menu, as well as being a part of the food offered in the more chic pubs and bistros throughout the country.

Roast Beef and Yorkshire Pudding

Not only is this a traditional British meal but the Yorkshire Pudding is traditional fayre in its own right, and needless to say a huge part of Yorkshire culture and tradition from where it is said to have originated during the Industrial Revolution. It was then that families, apparently realising they had little or no time to prepare a hearty meal after a visit to church, put a joint of meat into the oven to slow roast in their absence. In Yorkshire and some other Northern counties the Yorkshire Pudding is served first as a starter and a separate course. When, as a child, Maureen questioned her mother about this tradition she said that in lean times the Yorkshires were served before the meat to fill up the diners and so stop them eating too much of the more expensive meat. Maureen heard this many times and so assumed it to be true. She preferred her Yorkshires first, much to the amusement of her Southern friends and family.

The Full English Breakfast

If you are British you will no doubt have sampled a selection of these during your lifetime, in a manner of guises. The well-known bacon, egg, tomatoes, sausage, toast, beans and mushrooms is the envy of the world. The poor old Continentals have to put up with croissants and slices of cold ham and cheese. Nobody beats the quality of a full English breakfast, and although popular in the whole of the UK, it is also referred to as the British breakfast. But where did this now historical tradition come from?

Hundreds of years ago in agrarian Britain, poor farm labourers might start the day with some ale, bread and if they were lucky a little bit of beef. A selection of foods was the prerogative of the upper classes. However, the Industrial Revolution changed people's eating habits. From the mid-eighteenth century, the emerging factory working classes needed a hearty breakfast to see them through 12 hours of hard manual labour. It was at this time the Wiltshire farmers had imported Irish pigs and were developing their own pig-farming methods, whilst frying eggs and tomatoes was a well-known Chinese tradition and the rest just fell into place gradually. A full hot breakfast became the morning staple diet of the workshop of the world – Britain's factory and manufacturing culture. No longer was this the preserve of the wealthy upper classes.

The full English breakfast! (*Photo: Kieran Hughes*)

Today, thousands of cafes, homes, hospitals, hotels, pubs and restaurants serve a full English breakfast on a regular basis. However, not everyone is in agreement over this great British institution. Journalist James Ramsden, writing in the *Guardian* in 2013, called the dish 'a national disgrace'. He accused it of being 'overrated' and the 'scourge of the breakfast table'. He said, 'Even the name is shuddersome and unhealthy.' There are also some very expensive versions of this British dish. Jumeirah Carlton Hotel, the Ritz and the Dorchester, all in London, charge between £35 and £39 for one breakfast; the dish costs far less than £2 to make.

Ice Cream

Mr Whippy Ice Cream

British people have become obsessed with the Mr Whippy ice-cream product over the generations. Kieran had the pleasure of working in an ice-cream van one summer as a student. He observed that normally sane, well-educated, smartly dressed adults could turn into tantrum-throwing, jabbering idiots when they heard that the Mr Whippy machine was out of order or had run out. The bottom lip of grown men would actually protrude in a sulky, about to cry manner. People outside Britain do not have the same animal-like obsession for Mr Whippy. They seem to be quite happy with a scoop of ice cream in a cone, even if it doesn't come twirling out of a machine. Kieran is quite biased in his hatred of Mr Whippy machines, having spent hours in his youth cleaning them out, likening this to cleaning a cow field with the cow pats cemented on!

Ice-cream historian Steve Tillyear has written extensively about Mister Softee/Mr Whippy, about the history of ice cream and the different ice-cream vans from years gone by, including the unmistakable sound of the tonibell chimes. Brits take their ice cream very seriously, and are known for it and loved for it! Therefore, the most important development in the history of ice cream, way beyond the significance of any new flavours, was definitely the introduction of soft, whipped ice cream that dropped into the cone below. The method was discovered by a British chemical research team which decided to double the amount of air in ice cream, giving it the twirly and lighter texture. One of the young scientists who was part of that research body was the former British Prime Minister Margaret Thatcher. However, newyorker.com claims it was invented before she was part of the food research department at J. Lyons, branding the claims a complete myth.

Chasing the Ice-cream Van Down the Street

The tradition of the ice-cream van 'down our street' is not strictly a British custom, but it 'has' become part of our heritage. As a nation, we love our ice-cream vans. Even the most aggressive boy racers on the roads will sit patiently behind an ice-cream van taking the hill at the speed of an asthmatic snail on crutches. Loving our ice-cream man seems to be engrained in our psyche, perhaps giving subliminal flashbacks to a happy childhood.

Did You Know?

Fun Facts about Ice Cream

- King Tang of Shang had ninety-four ice-men who made him his favourite ice-cream treats on demand.
- The USA and China consume the most ice cream in the entire world.
- According to grandparents.com research, it takes an average of fifty licks to finish each scoop of ice cream.
- Ice cream first became available to the general public in France in 1660.
- The most popular flavour in the world is still vanilla, with chocolate serving as the runner-up.
- June is always the month that the most ice cream is produced.
- The ice-cream cone was first invented in 1904.

Favourite ice-cream quote:

'When I'm not longer rapping, I want to open up an ice-cream parlour and call myself Scoop Dogg.' – Snoop Dogg

There are some unusual laws governing mobile ice-cream vans in Britain. The musical chimes are limited to bursts of 4 seconds and must adhere to a 3-minute gap between bursts near schools, hospitals and churches. The schools and hospitals rule seems logical, but churches? These establishments are permitted to ring their bells for long periods of time early on a Sunday morning with no monitor on the excessive decibels being put out.

When Maureen was growing up in the 1970s in Shropshire, children could eat as much ice cream as could be afforded or was allowed. There were no fat children because they then ran around the fields for hours on end or went on their bikes, peddling until their legs felt like dropping off. Even the child who had the double chocolate sauce on his Mr Whippy never received the obesity lecture because he would burn off the calories instantly climbing trees or defying today's cotton-wool health and safety nanny state in every way possible – and guess what? He survived!

What Did We Get From the Ice-cream Van That Became Part of Our Lifelong Memories?

Screwballs seem to have started in the 1970s, in an upside-down, plastic, triangular cone. This was full of ice cream and topped with either sauce or hundreds and thousands. However, the biggest draw was the bubblegum ball everyone knew was nestling in the bottom, just waiting for us. **The Fab**, a classic from the 1960s that every child ate in a completely different way. **The Calippo**, really good on a hot day. You had to suck the hardened, flavoured iced water from the top, making the cardboard go soggy, which never tasted very nice but we loved it anyway.

A Cornetto. (*Photo: Kieran Hughes*)

Mini Milks were 'cheap' tiny lollies which never really tasted of milk but they came in three flavours: strawberry, vanilla and chocolate. **Cornettos** were only for the grown-ups or the richer kids at the ice-cream van. The best part was that huge chunk of chocolate waiting for you at the bottom of the cone.

'Ice Cream Ages' by David Harper

The ice cream van comes, I'm just three feet tall,
I look up but there's no way I can see at all,
Twister, Screwball, Cornet and Zoom,
I want it all and I have lots of room.
Ice Cream van comes and now I'm six feet tall
I look down to see what they all want,
Zapper, Magnum, Mini Milk and a Rocket,
I can buy them all as I now have a full pocket.
Ice cream van comes and I'm much older by far,
I look up but don't get what all these new names are,
Sparkles, Whippy and a row of sweets beneath,
I choose something soft, now I've lost all my teeth!

Chocolates and Sweets

Britain is a nation of sweet and chocolate lovers. This section takes a look as some of the greatest sweets and chocolates developed, manufactured and eaten in this country. Britain also boasts some of the world's best known confectioners such as Cadbury's, Terry's and Rowntree's, which are also discussed in this section.

A Brief History of Sweets

- It is thought that the peppermint-flavoured humbug sweet dates from as far back as the early nineteenth century, although an exact date is difficult to establish. The old man's favourite has been enjoyed by all ages for more than 200 years.
- In 1881, the Rowntree family developed the Fruit Pastille and started to make them in Tyneside.
- Liquorice Allsorts date back to 1899 when a liquorice salesman was showing a tray of the sweets to a prospective client, all lined up on a tray in colour order but then dropped them all over the floor. The customer commented on how nice the jumbled up 'mixture' of colours looked. The salesmen took the idea back to his boss and the multi-coloured Liquorice Allsorts idea was born!
- In the early 1900s, Charles Maynard invented the wine gum as a way of appealing to sweet-toothed adults but without offending his tee-total father.
- In 1918, British sweet manufacturer Bassett's decided to create little coloured sweet men to commemorate the end of the First World War. They were relaunched as Jelly Babies in the 1950s and have remained one of the nation's favourites. Many grown men still feel guilty about biting off the head first!
- In 1925 Barratt's launched the Sherbet Fountain with the liquorice stick immersed in a yellow tube of sherbet. Perhaps one of the messiest sweets of its day, it has been enjoyed by many a child over the last ninety-three years.
- Blackjack chews used to feature the smiling face of a golliwog until the 1980s when this was dropped. Many adults can remember having a black tongue drowning in aniseed flavour.

- The Polo Mint was born in 1948 after its 1939 launch date was cancelled as a result of the Second World War.
- Swizzels-Matlow originally produced Love Hearts in Christmas crackers in the 1950s. However, the super sweet, tongue-tingling treats soon made it onto the regular confectionery shelves, with their little messages on them, for example, 'Ever Yours' and 'Kiss Me'.
- Opal Fruits hit the shops in the early 1960s, produced by Mars Confectionery. By the 1990s they were renamed Starburst (the American brand name). Today they are owned by Wrigley.
- The Flying Saucer was launched in the 1960s, as two tasteless discs of coloured rice paper encasing a tiny amount of sherbet. One of the most popular sweets in Britain ever but the rice paper simply tasted of newspaper!

Terry's Chocolate

British chocolate and sweet maker Terry's was founded in York in 1767 by Robert Berry. One of his relatives, Joseph Terry, joined the business and eventually became the sole owner, renaming it Terry's of York, in 1828. By the 1920s, as business expanded, the company bought a site in Bishopthorpe Road, York, on which to develop a new factory known as Terry's Confectionery Works. Five years after the factory opened Terry's Chocolate Orange was made there for the first time, and Terry's All Gold was added to the portfolio. After the Second World War the company struggled because of rationing and import difficulties. There were a number of different owners of the business over the following years, ending with the purchase by Kraft Foods in 1993. From 2000, the company brand was changed from Terry's of York to Terry's, distancing itself from the city of York where it had all begun. In September 2005, after more than a century of chocolate making, Terry's factory closed its Bishopthorpe Road doors for the last time. Production of Terry's chocolate in Britain was eventually moved abroad to countries such as Poland, Sweden, Belgium and Slovakia. The owners recognised that many of the employees had worked there for their entire career, and in some cases their parents and grandparents.

Rowntree's Chocolate

In 1862, Quaker businessman Henry Isaac Rowntree purchased the Tukes' cocoa and chocolate business in York. He liked the idea of socially drinking chocolate as an alternative to alcohol for the working man. In 1869 he was joined in the business by his brother, Joseph Rowntree. By 1881 the firm began the manufacture of pastilles, helped by a French confectioner. As the business expanded, they moved to a 24-acre site in 1890. At the start of the twentieth century, its popular Elect Cocoa product was declining in sales. Further hit by the Depression in the 1920s, the company's marketing director George Harris focused on product development, branding and advertising, launching KitKat, Aero, Dairy Box, Smarties and Rolos in the 1930s. Rowntree's became York's biggest employer, with 14,000 workers.

When the factory bell rang at the end of a shift, thousands of workers streamed out on bicycles, dominating the traffic and taking over the city's roads. Both of Maureen's parents worked at Rowntree's. In the 1960s and 1970s the factory policy was that workers could eat as much chocolate as they wanted. The policy was a great success because most workers ate so much chocolate when they started they could not face eating it ever again,

The Rowntree's factory in York. (*Image supplied by David Benson*)

thus practically eliminating theft. Another treat workers enjoyed was the right to buy huge bags of imperfect chocolate for a token few pence. In 1988, Swiss multinational Nestlé bought Rowntree's against a backdrop of local opposition.

Cadbury's Chocolate

In 1824, John Cadbury opened a grocer's shop in Birmingham, selling cocoa and drinking chocolate. By 1842 John was selling sixteen varieties of drinking chocolate and eleven different cocoas. Later, he developed chocolate eggs and by 1879 work had started on the construction of a new Cadbury factory in Birmingham. By now, John's sons, Richard and George, were in charge and determined to create a pleasurable working environment at their chocolate factory instead of the usual grim industrial surroundings. They built dozens of houses and created leisure facilities for their workers. Meanwhile, Cadbury milk chocolate hit the shelves in 1897, made of

John Cadbury, *c.* 1840s.

Cadbury's factory in Edwardian times. (*Image courtesy of David Benson*)

milk powder paste, cocoa mass, cocoa butter and sugar, quite coarse and dry and not very sweet. The quality of chocolate had improved by 1915, and the first really affordable box of chocolates was produced by Cadbury's, called Milk Tray. Before this, a box of chocolates was a very expensive treat that could only be purchased by the better off. In 1948, the Fudge bar was launched, the Creme Egg in 1971 and the Wispa in 1981. In 1969 Cadbury's merged with Schweppes.

Chapter 4

Royalty

Many British people are fiercely proud of the royal family and the tourists are fiercely curious and so it seems only fitting that we start with the 'possession' of which we are most proud.

The British Royal Family

Prince Philip calls the royal family 'The Firm', as though it is some sort of commodity and let's face it, in the cold light of day that is exactly what it is, a commodity that plays a huge and significant part in enticing tourists to Great Britain, so in fact more than paying its way as a part of the British economy. Let's take a look at this 'Firm'.

Her Majesty Queen Elizabeth II

Born in 1926, the eldest daughter of the future King George VI and Queen Elizabeth, formerly Lady Elizabeth Bowes-Lyon, she herself became Queen at the tender age of 25. In 1947 she married Prince Philip and together they have had four children. Throughout her reign she has been a calming influence on the often turbulent monarchy and is head of state of the UK. There are sixteen nations in the Commonwealth which share Queen Elizabeth II as their Head of State. In 2015 she became the longest serving monarch in British history, finally overtaking Queen Victoria. Her Majesty is the only person in the country who does not have to hold a passport to travel abroad. Neither does she have to display a registration number on her car. In fact, the reigning monarch does not have to hold a valid driving licence. As an 18-year-old princess she joined the Women's Auxiliary Territorial Service during the Second World War and trained as a mechanic and military truck driver. To this day, Queen Elizabeth is the only female (British) royal to have served in the armed forces. In addition, she is the only living head of state who served in the Second World War. In 1976 she became the first head of state to send an email, as she took part in trials for this new information technology. Queen Elizabeth is also known for being very composed and measured. In 1981 when a youth fired six blanks at her during a horse parade, she simply calmed down her shaken horse and proceeded with the procession, letting police deal with the gunman. That was nothing compared with an incident that took place on the night of 9 July 1982, when a lone intruder made it all the way into her bedroom, having climbed up a drainpipe. Her Majesty simply kept him talking for 10 minutes, asking him lots of questions about his family. In the end a footman came to her rescue.

His Royal Highness the Duke of Edinburgh

The Duke of Edinburgh was born in Corfu on 10 June 1921 as Prince Philip of Greece and Denmark, the only son of Prince Andrew of Greece and the grandson of King Christian IX of Denmark. Not only is the Duke of Edinburgh well known as the husband of Queen Elizabeth II, who according to royal protocol he has been obliged to walk two paces behind since she became Queen, but he is also well known for his infamous gaffes. These faux pas have endeared him to the British public and become a part of his charm. The Queen is elegance personified and her husband is 'amusing', as demonstrated by the following list of comments made by the Duke:

- To the President of Nigeria, who was in national dress: 'You look like you're ready for bed!'
- To a tourist in Budapest: 'You can't have been here long, you haven't got a pot belly.'
- On the Duke of York's house: 'It looks like a tart's bedroom.'
- To Cayman Islanders: 'Aren't most of you descended from pirates?'
- To a Scottish driving instructor: 'How do you keep the natives off the booze long enough to pass the test?'

There is a full list of his howlers in the book *The Pocket Guide to Royal Scandals*, by Andy K. Hughes (2011).

His Royal Highness Prince Charles Philip Arthur George, Prince of Wales
Or to give him his full title – His Royal Highness Prince Charles Philip Arthur George, Prince of Wales, KG, KT, GCB, OM, AK, QSO, PC, ADC, Earl of Chester, Duke of Cornwall, Duke of Rothesay, Earl of Carrick, Baron of Renfrew, Lord of the Isles and Prince and Great Steward of Scotland. Prince Charles, as he is more simply known, is the first born of Queen Elizabeth II and next in line to the British throne. He was educated, as his father before him, at Gordonstoun School in Moray, Scotland, where the emphasis is on developing its students for their place in an international world, a world where one day they can perhaps make a difference. The school's motto is '*Plus est en Vous*' – 'There is more in you (than you think)'.

At the time of going to print this was the current line of succession to the British throne, according to britroyals.com:

1. HRH Prince Charles, The Prince of Wales (b. 1948).
2. HRH Prince William of Wales, The Duke of Cambridge (b. 1982).
3. HRH Prince George of Cambridge (b. 2013).
4. HRH Princess Charlotte of Cambridge (b. 2015).
5. HRH Prince Henry of Wales (Harry) (b. 1984).
6. HRH Prince Andrew, The Duke of York (b. 1960).
7. HRH Princess Beatrice of York (b. 1988).
8. HRH Princess Eugenie of York (b. 1990).
9. HRH Prince Edward (b. 1964).
10. James, Viscount Severn (b. 2007).
11. Lady Louise Windsor (b. 2003).
12. HRH Princess Anne, Princess Royal (b. 1950) .
13. Peter Phillips (b. 1977).
14. Savannah Phillips (b. 2010).
15. Isla Phillips (b. 2012).
16. Zara Tindall (Phillips) (b. 1981).
17. Mia Grace Tindall (b. 2014).
18. David Armstrong-Jones, Viscount Linley (b. 1961).
19. Hon. Charles Armstrong-Jones (b. 1999).
20. Margarita Armstrong-Jones (b. 2002).

21. Lady Sarah Chatto (b. 1964).
22. Samuel Chatto (b. 1996).
23. Arthur Chatto (b. 1999).
24. HRH Prince Richard, Duke of Gloucester (b. 1944).
25. Alexander Windsor, Earl of Ulster (b. 1974).
26. Xan Windsor, Lord Culloden (b. 2007).
27. Lady Cosima Windsor (b. 2010).
28. Lady Davina Lewis (b. 1977).
29. Senna Lewis (b. 2010).
30. Tane Mahuta Lewis (b. 2012).
31. Lady Rose Gilman (b. 1980).
32. Lyla Gilman (b. 2010).
33. Rufus Gilman (b. 2012).
34. HRH Prince Edward, Duke of Kent (b. 1935).
35. George Windsor, Earl of St Andrews (b. 1962).
    Edward Windsor, Baron Downpatrick (excluded by becoming a Roman Catholic).
    Lady Marina Charlotte Windsor (excluded by becoming a Roman Catholic).
36. Lady Amelia Windsor (b. 1995).
    Lord Nicholas Windsor (excluded by becoming a Roman Catholic).
    Albert Windsor (excluded by being Roman Catholic).
    Leopold Windsor (excluded by being Roman Catholic).
    Louis Windsor (excluded by being Roman Catholic).
37. Lady Helen Taylor (b. 1964).
38. Columbus Taylor (b. 1994).
39. Cassius Taylor (b. 1996).
40. Eloise Taylor (b. 2003).
41. Estella Taylor (b. 2004).
42. Prince Michael of Kent (b. 1942).
43. Lord Frederick Windsor (b. 1979).
44. Maud Windsor (b. 2013).
45. Isabella Windsor (b. 2016).
46. Lady Gabriella Windsor (b. 1981).
47. HRH Princess Alexandra the Hon. Lady Ogilvy (b. 1936).

48. James Ogilvy (b. 1964).
49. Alexander Ogilvy (b. 1996).
50. Flora Ogilvy (b. 1994).
51. Marina Ogilvy, Mrs Paul Mowatt (b. 1966).
52. Christian Mowatt (b. 1993).
53. Miss Zenouska Mowatt (b. 1990).
54. David Lascelles, 8th Earl of Harewood (b. 1950).
55. Hon. Alexander Lascelles (b. 1980).
56. Hon. Edward Lascelles (b. 1982).
57. Hon. James Lascelles (b. 1953).
58. Rowan Lascelles (b. 1977).
59. Tewa Lascelles (b. 1985).
60. Sophie Lascelles (b. 1973).
61. Hon. Jeremy Lascelles (b. 1955).
62. Thomas Lascelles (b. 1982).
63. Ellen Lascelles (b. 1984).
64. Amy Lascelles (b. 1986).
65. Tallulah Lascelles (b. 2005).
66. Henry Lascelles (b. 1953).
67. Maximilian Lascelles (b. 1991).
68. David Carnegie, 4th Duke of Fife (b. 1961).
69. Lord Charles Duff Carnegie (b. 1989).
70. Hon. George William Carnegie (b. 1991).
71. Hon. Hugh Alexander Carnegie (b. 1993).
72. Lady Alexandra Etherington (b. 1959).
73. Amelia Mary Carnegie Etherington (b. 2001).
74. HM King Harald V of Norway (b. 1937).
75. HRH Crown Prince Haakon of Norway (b. 1973).
76. HH Prince Sverre Magnus of Norway (b. 2005).
77. HRH Princess Ingrid Alexandra of Norway (b. 2004).
78. Princess Martha Louise of Norway (b. 1971).
79. Maud Angelica Behn (b. 2003).
80. Leah Isadora Behn (b. 2005).
81. Emma Talullah Behn (b. 2008).
82. Haakon Lorentzen (b. 1954).

83. Olav Lorentzen (b. 1985).
84. Christian Lorentzen (b. 1988).
85. Sophia Lorentzen (b. 1994).
86. Ingeborg Ribeiro (b. 1957).
87. Victoria Ribeiro (b. 1988).
88. Ragnhild Lorentzen Long (b. 1968).
89. Alexandra Lorentzen Long (b. 2007).
90. Elizabeth Lorentzen Long (b. 2011).
91. HH Princess Astrid of Norway (b. 1932).
92. Alexander Ferner (b. 1965).
93. Stella Ferner (b. 1998).
94. Carl-Christian Ferner (b. 1972).
95. Cathrine Johansen (b. 1962).
96. Sebastian Johansen (b. 1990).
97. Madeleine Johansen (b. 1993).
98. Benedikte Ferner (b. 1963).
99. Elisabeth Ferner Beckman (b. 1969).
100. Benjamin Ferner Beckman (b. 1999).

Positions exclude births after May 2017. The Succession of the Crown Act, 2013, ended discrimination based on gender or 'marrying' a Roman Catholic.

Royal Residences

'An Englishman's home is his castle'

A lovely saying, but true of course only generally in the case of the royal family, for the rest of us mere mortals live in more modest accommodation. Royal residences are not just homes but are in fact multi-purpose buildings and so, as well as each being a family home, they also house working offices for the staff of the Royal Household and they could also be described as restaurants too, bearing in mind the amount of entertaining the Queen is obliged to do as a part of her 'job' as Head of State. Let us first take a look at the two most famous royal residences, Buckingham Palace and Windsor Castle.

Buckingham Palace

Buckingham Palace is probably the most famous royal residence in the world. It has been the official London residence of Britain's sovereigns since 1837. Today it is not only the home of the British reigning monarch but is also the administrative headquarters of the monarchy, bringing a whole new meaning to the saying 'working from home'! In Buckingham Palace there are the offices of those who support the day-to-day activities and duties of the Queen, the Duke of Edinburgh and their immediate family.

As if working from home wasn't bad enough, how would the rest of us feel if we had to endure hoards of complete strangers wandering around our house and passing comment on everything they see? For that is just what the royal family has to do in today's economic climate, for just such a venture as opening a royal residence to the general public brings in an enormous amount of money to the royal coffers. Of course, it is only the state rooms that are open to the public and not the Queen's private rooms. Whilst the rest of us may panic in the run up to Christmas, or family birthdays, both of which can herald the arrival of the extended family in their droves, being a member of the Royal family is entirely different for they are obliged to entertain, by comparison, on a huge and magnificent scale, people they may never have met before and possibly will never meet again.

Balmoral Castle

Prince Albert first leased and then bought the building and later the surrounding land as a gift for Queen Victoria between 1848 and 1852. Balmoral Castle subsequently became the Scottish home of the royal family. It all started in 1842 when Queen Victoria paid her first visit to Scotland and fell in love with the beauty of the Highlands. She later paid visits to Perthshire and Ardverikie and vowed to return to Scotland again. Once Prince Albert had purchased the surrounding land, he went about rebuilding the current house which he felt was not fit for the needs of a royal family. The building site of the new castle was only a hundred yards from the old building. The foundation stone was laid by Queen Victoria on 28 September 1853 and the castle was completed in 1856; the old building was then demolished.

Clarence House
Situated in Central London beside St James's Palace, Clarence House will always be known by the British people as the home of the late Queen Mother.

Frogmore
Situated in Windsor and purchased for Queen Charlotte in 1792, Frogmore House is no longer used as a royal residence. It was a favourite getaway for Queen Victoria (especially during her mourning) and Queen Elizabeth II has often used it for entertaining. In fact, the house was the location for the wedding of her eldest grandson, Peter Phillips, in 2008.

Kensington Palace
Situated in Central London, Kensington Palace is home to many members of the royal family who live in the luxurious private apartments of the palace. Kensington Palace was the birthplace and childhood home of Queen Victoria.

Palace of Holyroodhouse
Situated in Edinburgh, Scotland, Holyroodhouse is the Queen's official residence in Scotland and is where she and the Duke of Edinburgh entertain about 8,000 guests each year. Mary, Queen of Scots, lived here between 1561 and 1567.

Sandringham House
Sandringham House in Norfolk has been the country home of four British monarchs since 1862. The house and gardens are open to the public, as well as a museum.

St James's Palace
Situated in Central London, St James's Palace is not open to the public.

Fascinating Royal Facts

- There are 775 rooms in Buckingham Palace; these include 19 state rooms, 52 royal and guest bedrooms, 188 staff bedrooms, 92 offices and 78 bathrooms.
- The royal family is known and admired for their love of animals and the Queen is famously often accompanied by her beloved corgis.
- Many members of the royal family are accomplished horse riders, even representing the country at the Olympics.
- The Queen, as the Queen Mother before her, loves horse racing, whilst the Duke of Edinburgh became a trophy winning carriage driver after taking up the sport in the 1970s.
- Investitures, of which there are usually 21 a year – 9 in spring, 2 in the summer and 10 in the autumn – are usually held in the Ballroom of Buckingham Palace.
- Four royal babies – the Prince of Wales, the Princess Royal, the Duke of York and Prince William – were all christened by the Archbishop of Canterbury in the Music Room at Buckingham Palace.
- It can sometimes be difficult to work out exactly where the Queen lives, but generally it is as follows:
  - When working – unless overseas – she divides her time between London and Windsor.
  - Every year she spends a week in Edinburgh – this is called Holyrood Week.
  - Holidays are spent at Balmoral Castle, Aberdeenshire, or Sandringham House, Norfolk.
- Every Tuesday the Queen is visited by the Prime Minister of the day.
- The Queen's full birth name – that is the name she was christened – is Elizabeth Alexandra Mary of York.
- The Queen married the Duke of Edinburgh on 20 November 1947.
- Queen Elizabeth II is Britain's longest serving monarch throughout history.

Pomp and Ceremony – It's What We Do Best!

The British are known throughout the world for their national traditions, which in many cases date back hundreds of years, and the moment that there is a national event warranting pomp and splendour then people from across the globe flock to British shores to witness it for themselves, and guess what? They are never disappointed, for pomp and ceremony is what the British do best.

Some of the key national events are the state opening of Parliament, Trooping the Colour and royal weddings. Nothing can be more certain of attracting tourists to Britain in their thousands than a good royal wedding. For this is when the flags fly, the carriages roll and the tears flow! And everyone is happy. There have been two spectacular royal weddings in the last fifty years that stand out amongst the others – of which there have been quite a few – and those are the weddings of Prince Charles and Lady Diana Spencer and Prince William and Kate Middleton.

Kings and Queens Who Ruled Parts of England, England as a Whole and Britain in its Entirety

- Athelstan (924–39).
- Edmund I (939–46).
- Edred (946–55).
- Edwy the Fair (955–9).
- Edgar the Peaceable (959–75).
- St Edward the Martyr (975–8).
- Ethelred the Unready (978–1013, 1014–16), interrupted by Sweyn Forkbeard.
- Edmund Ironside (1016).

Danish Kings
- Canute the Great (1016–35).
- Harold Harefoot (1035–40).
- Harthacnut (1040–2).

Wessex Kings
- Edward the Confessor (1042–66).
- Harold Godwinson (1066).

Normans
- William the Conqueror (1066–87).
- William II (1087–1100).
- Henry I (1100–35).
- Stephen (1135–54), also House of Blois.

Plantagenets
- Empress Matilda (1141), disputed.
- Henry II (1154–89).
- Richard I, the Lionheart (1189–99).
- John (1199–1216).
- Henry III (1216–72).
- Edward I (1272–1307).
- Edward II (1307–27; deposed, died 1327).
- Edward III (1327–77).
- Richard II (1377–99; deposed, died 1400).

Lancastrians
- Henry IV (1399–1413).
- Henry V (1413–22).
- Henry VI (1422–61 and 1470–1).

Yorkists
- Edward IV (1461–70 and 1471–83).
- Edward V (uncrowned) (1483; deposed 1483, possibly assassinated).
- Richard III (1483–5).

Tudors
- Henry VII (1485–1509).
- Henry VIII (1509–47).
- Edward VI (1547–53).
- Jane (1553; beheaded 1554).
- Mary I (1553–8).
- Elizabeth I (1558–1603).

Stuarts
In personal union with England until 1707.

- James I (1603–25), also from 1567 King James VI of Scotland.
- Charles I (1625–49), also King of Scotland.

Interregnum
There was a civil war in England from 1642 until 1651. In 1649, King Charles I was executed and England became a Commonwealth. It lasted until 1660 when the monarchy was restored.

Stuarts
- Charles II (1660–85), also King of Scotland (backdated the start of his reign to 1649).
- James II (1685–8; deposed, died 1701), also King James VII of Scotland.
- William III (1689–1702) and Mary II (1689–94), as co-monarchs, also King and Queen of Scotland.
- Anne (1702–14), though the English throne was replaced with that of the Kingdom of Great Britain in 1707.

House of Hanover
- George I (1714–27).
- George II (1727–60).
- George III (1760–1801).
- George III (1801–20).
- George IV (1820–30; Regent 1811–20).
- William IV (1830–7).
- Victoria (1837–1901).

House of Saxe-Coburg and Gotha
The royal household changed its name to Saxe-Coburg-Gotha after Queen Victoria married Prince Albert of Saxe-Coburg-Gotha, but Victoria remained part of the House of Hanover. The name was not changed until 1917 by George V.

- Edward VII (1901–10).

House of Windsor
- George V (1910–21; changed name of house in 1917 as the former name sounded German and Britain was at war with Germany).
- George V (1921–36).
- Edward VIII (1936; abdicated).
- George VI (1936–52).
- Elizabeth II (1952–present).

Chapter 5

Alternative Royalty – Pearly Kings And Queens

In Great Britain we have another set of 'Kings and Queens' who have nothing at all to do with the royal family, but who are nevertheless a very important part of British heritage, and they are the Pearly Kings and Queens.

As a child in Yorkshire Maureen was brought up to believe that the Pearly Kings and Queens – otherwise known as the Pearlies – were very special people who were to be respected for the good works they did. However, she was aware that they always dressed in very individual clothes that were adorned with pearly buttons. She never questioned the respect she was told to have for them, but just accepted it and so when it came to writing this book on Great Britain it was only natural to include these 'special' people.

The Pearlies are in fact figureheads for the working class communities of London. Unlike the royal family in Great Britain with either just one king or one queen as the ruling monarch of the day, within the Pearlie community it is quite different altogether, for each London Borough, including the City of London and the City of Westminster, has its very own Pearly King and Queen – and of course all the little Pearly Princes and Princesses too!

Where and When Did it All Begin?

The Pearly community as whole was founded in the year 1875 by Henry Croft (1862–1930). Henry Croft was raised in a Victorian workhouse orphanage in Charles Street, in London's St Pancras; a more grim and difficult start to life is hard to imagine. At the age of 13, and as was normal at the time, he left the orphanage to start earning his own living, which in his case was as a road sweeper and rat catcher. It was during his time as a road sweeper that Henry became fascinated by a group of Londoners called costermongers.

The Costermongers

The costermongers were a group of people who bought fruit and vegetables wholesale and sold them retail. Generally they did not work from fixed market stalls, but instead cried out their wares and sold life's essentials as they walked the streets of London with barrows, donkey carts or trays carried on their heads. They were a tough bunch of people and as Henry got to know more about their way of life he found that he was particularly drawn to their clothing, which featured pearl buttons sewn onto the piped seams of trousers, jackets, waistcoats and caps. He found the costermongers to be caring folk who looked after each other if they were sick or in need, personality traits that must have seemed very endearing to a child brought up in a Victorian orphanage. It was, in fact, this attitude that he witnessed in the costermongers' own community that inspired his desire to collect money for those less fortunate than himself.

Henry decided to take the suit decorations used by the costermongers and which he so admired one step further by decorating an entire suit, including top hat and tails, in pearl buttons. And so it was that the Pearlies, at this point, started to evolve and Henry himself, as a result, became the centre of attention wherever he went. So the young Henry, who was barely more than a child himself, went out dressed from head to foot in clothes adorned with pearly buttons collecting pennies and halfpennies to help children in the orphanage where he himself was raised as a child. His popularity grew and so hospitals and other organised bodies asked him to collect for the deaf, dumb and blind; Henry's celebrated lifetime of charity work had begun but he needed help to continue with his charity work and that help came from the very people who had been his initial inspiration, the costermongers.

A small child's fascination with costermongers and their way of dressing combined with a desire to help the poor then grew into the more flamboyant Pearly community that we know today, with its own monarchy and where all community members wear the ornate and eyecatching mode of dress. In addition, many of the costers became Pearly families too. The Pearlies then went on to become a tourist attraction not just with Londoners themselves but with visitors from all over Great Britain. As travel became easier, foreign tourists also wanted to see the 'other' monarchy. In fact, all sorts of people wanted to see this group of eccentrically dressed folk who also did good works for the less than fortunate. The wonderful thing is, of course, that as the new Pearly community grew, then so too did their charity work as they went on to embrace and help many more different causes that needed help. For that reason, 'Long live the pearly kings and queens'.

Where to See the Pearlies

As a much respected part of the London community, visitors often arrive in London expecting to see the Pearly Kings and Queens as often as the more traditional sights. Sometimes tourists seem disappointed not to see them wandering around the streets, but then the royal family don't wander around the streets of London and so why would the Pearlies? The less accessible and the more mysterious a person becomes, then the more intriguing they become too, and when charity work is involved then that probably is not a bad thing.

If you do want to see the Pearlies there are two very colourful events in their calendar year where this is possible: the Pearly Memorial Service, which is held every year on the third Sunday of May, and the harvest festival service, which is held on the first Sunday in October. Both of these events are held at St Martin-in-the-Fields, Trafalgar Square, London and the Pearly Kings and Queens, Princes and Princesses, young and old, turn out in all their wonderfully decorated finery. A parade of Pearly Kings and Queens was also featured at the 2012 Summer Olympics Opening Ceremony. In the Crypt of St Martin-in-the-Fields you can also see a life-size memorial statue of Henry Croft in his fine top hat and tails pearly suit. This statue was donated by the hospitals, societies and other charitable organisations that Henry had helped in his lifetime – the inscription reads:

In memory of Henry Croft who died
March 16th 1930 aged 68 years
The original Pearly King

The following table gives details of past and current Pearlies.

Pearly Kings, Queens, Princes and Princesses

Location	Name	Title
Acton	Pat Hannan (deceased)	Queen
Bank Side and Bow Bells	Tom Johnson (deceased)	King
Barnet	Jack Hammond Brenda Hammond	King Queen
Battersea	William Emmings Emily Emmings	King Queen
Battersea (now living in Australia)	Harold State (deceased) Alice James Rowan State	King Queen King (son)
Bethnal Green	Bill Morris Martha Morris	King Queen
Bethnal Green	Glen Arrowsmith	King
Blackheath	Don Jolly (deceased) Dorothy Jolly (retired)	King Queen
Borough	Jack James	King
Borough (The)	Bert Lodge	King
Bow Bells and Blackfriars	Harry Mayhead Bow Bells (title given by Tommy Johnson's family)	King
Brent	Charlie Harman Pam Harman John Harman	King Queen Prince
Camberwell	Jimmy Jukes Dee Russell	King Queen
Camden	George Smith Rose Matthew-Smith	King Queen
Canning Town	June Cartwright (deceased)	Queen
Chelsea	Bill West (deceased)	King
Chingford	Sheila Arrowsmith	Queen

Location	Name	Title
City of London	George Hitchen (deceased) Sadie Hitchen (deceased) Arthur Hitchen	King Queen Prince
City of London	Vic Nutley Hailey Friend Grant Nutley	King Queen Prince
Clapton	Theresa Watts Alfie Watts	Queen Prince
Crowborough	David Hemsley James Hemsley Sophie Hemsley	King Prince Princess
Croydon	Samantha Bissett Lucy Bissett Billy Bissett	Queen Princess Prince
Crystal Palace	Pat Jolly Carole Jolly Rebecca Jolly	King Queen Princess
Dagenham	Albert Singfield Rose Singfield	King Queen
Dalston	Ronnie Nutley	King
Dover	Bill Bliss	King
Dulwich	Fred Booth Maria Booth	King Queen
Ealing	Wayne Kebell	King
Edmonton	Mr Turner Mrs Turner (passed the title to Mary Armitage)	King Queen
Essex	Francis Adolphus Caulfield	Royal Pearly King
Finsbury	Marie Rackley	Queen
Finsbury	John Walters Kathy Walters Darren Walters	King Queen Prince
Fulham	Eddie Cheer (deceased) Flo Cheer	King Queen
Greenwich	Gwen Jones	Queen

Location	Name	Title
Greenwich, Deptford and Margate	Kitty Pinard	Queen
Grove Park	Alan Baxter Ginny Baxter Eden Baxter	King Queen Princess
Hackney	Alfred Meader Mrs Meader (passed title to Paul and Janet Groves)	King Queen
Hackney	Paul Groves Janet Groves	King Queen
Hackney	Mick Murphy (deceased) Jackie Murphy Lucy, Amy and Scarlet Crow	King Queen Princesses
Hammersmith	Steve Keeble	King
Hampstead	Ted Mathews Emily Mathews	King Queen
Hampstead	Linda Carter	Queen
Harrow	Brian Hemsley Margaret Hemsley	King Queen
Highgate	John Scott Peggy Scott	King Queen
Holloway	Mike Statwick Lily Statwick	King Queen
Homerton	Sharon Crow	Queen
Hornchurch	Natasha Caulfield	Queen
Hornsey	John Hannon	King
Hoxton	Clara West	Queen
Hoxton	Victor Nutley Philippa Nutley	King Queen
Hoxton	Vanessa Nutley	Queen
Isle of Dogs (Poplar)	Chris Friend Joan Friend Carol Nutley C.J. Friend	King Queen Princess Prince

Location	Name	Title
Islington	Lizzy Cole (no longer active)	Queen
Islington	Ernie Broadbent Phyllis Broadbent Robert Broadbent	King Queen Prince
Kensington and Chelsea	Dawn James Tony James Kate James	Queen King Princess
Kentish Town	Mr Pomeroy Mrs Pomeroy	King Queen
Kentish Town	John Caulfield	King
Kenton	George Edward Ralph	King
Lambeth	Edward (Wiggy) Marriott Jessie Marriott Daniel Dawn and Toni Marriott	King Queen Prince Princesses
Lambeth	Steve Smith Kerry Smith	King Queen
Leyton	Gerry Arrowsmith Helen Arrowsmith	King Queen
Leytonstone	Victor Arrowsmith Sandra Arrowsmith	King Queen
London	Beatrice Marriott Jean O'Shea	Festival Queen Princess
Marylebone	Andrew Baxter	King
Merton	John Brown Geraldine Brown	King Queen
New Cross and Old Kent Road	Larry Golding (deceased) Doreen Golding	King Queen
Newham	William George Davison Beatrice Ann Davison	King Queen
Newham	George Davison Angela Davison	King Queen
Norbury	Lola Gibbard Amy Gibbard Daniel Gibbard	Queen Princess Prince

Location	Name	Title
North Kensington	Ronald Montague Betty Montague	King Queen
Oxford	G.M. Shepherd	Queen
Pimlico	Sid Seymour (deceased) Dot Seymour (deceased)	King Queen
Portsmouth	Barry Seymour Dolly Seymour	King Queen
Redbridge	Peggy Oliver	Queen
Romford	Peter Caulfield Margaret Caulfield	King Queen
St Pancras	Tom Cooper Violet Cooper Tommy and Tony Cooper	King Queen Princes
St Pancras	Alfred Dole Mary Robinson Diane Martin (daughter) Maria Dole (niece)	King Queen Princess Princess
Shepherds Bush	Ron Keeble Dot Keeble Nicola Keeble	King Queen Princess
Shoreditch	Linda Murphy	Queen
Smithfield Market	Roy York Lily York	King Queen
Somers Town	Henry Croft (founder)	King
Somers Town	Steve Devereux Donna Devereux (great-granddaughter of Henry Croft) Milly Devereux Livvy Devereux	King Queen Princess Princess
Southwark	Fred Tinsley Mrs Tinsley	King Queen
Southwark	George Carr Joy Carr	King Queen
South-West London	John Smith Grace Smith	King Queen

Location	Name	Title
Stepney	Joe Kennedy Sylvia Kennedy Tony Kennedy Coleen Kennedy	King Queen Prince Princess
Stevenage	William T. Montague Kate E. Montague	King Queen
Stevenage	Jack James	King
Stoke Newington	Robert Springfield Rose Springfield Jean Springfield	King Queen Princess
Stonebridge	Kate James	Queen
Streatham	Gerry Baxter Kim Baxter Jen Baxter	King Queen Princess
Sydenham	Stephanie Jolly	Queen
Thornton Heath	Larry Barnes (deceased)	King
Tottenham	Harry Tongue Shirley Tongue Stephen Tongue	King Queen Prince
Tower Hamlets	Lorraine Wells	Queen
Upminster	Arthur Rackley	King
Upton park	Christine Prosser	Queen
Uxbridge	Arthur Henry Down Ellen Victoria Down	King Queen
Victoria	Sonny Plaw Carole Plaw Nicki Plaw Toni Plaw Billy Plaw	King Queen Princess Princess Princess
Walthamstow	Jon Arrowsmith Josette Kerrison	King Queen
Walworth	Mrs Tolhurst Betty Tolhurst	Queen Princess
Wandsworth	Edward Larkin	King
Wapping	Jim Davidson (deceased) Barbara Davidson	King Queen

Location	Name	Title
Waterloo	Jon Smith Sue Smith Barry and Adam Smith	King Queen Princes
Welwyn Garden City	Edie Marshall (deceased) Nicola (grand-daughter)	Queen Queen
Wembley	Terry Harman	King
West Ham	George Munns May Munns	King Queen
Westminster	Fred Hitchen (deceased) Lou Hitchen (deceased)	King Queen
Westminster	David Hitchen Kelly Hitchen James Hitchen	King Queen Prince
Whitechapel	Darren Arrowsmith	King
Willesdon	Fred Hall Mabel Hall	King Queen
Willesdon	Peter Harman	King
Wood Green	Chris Elliott Linda Elliott	King Queen
Woolwich	Clive Bennett	King
Woolwich	Sarah Golden (passed the title to the Hayes family)	Queen
Woolwich	Arthur Hayes (deceased) Emmy Hayes (deceased)	King Queen

The Pearly motto is: 'One Never Knows'.

Chapter 6

Places of Interest

Durham Cathedral

Durham World Heritage Site is located in the North-East of England. This stunning Norman cathedral was built between 1093 and 1133 in the Romanesque style. There was already a church on this site but the new cathedral was designed to replace it. The cathedral was originally built to house the shrine of St Cuthbert and to provide a monastic cathedral for a community of Benedictine monks. However, it later served as a vital political-military stronghold to reinforce the authority of the prince-bishops over England's northern border. These religious leaders ruled the Diocese of Durham from 1080 until 1836. Until 1603 they governed a near autonomous state with secular powers which created a safe zone between England and Scotland.

Durham Cathedral exterior in all its splendour. (*Photo: Hugh Mothersole*)

In 1539, the priory and monastic community were dissolved and surrendered to the Crown during the Reformation in the time of King Henry VIII. However, by May 1541 the cathedral was re-founded. *The Rites of Durham* (1591) is a useful source of valuable information about life in the cathedral before the Dissolution. The cathedral continued its chequered existence during the Civil War when it was closed for worship and used by Cromwell to imprison 3,000 Scottish soldiers after the Battle of Dunbar in 1650. By the nineteenth century, much of the stained glass windows in the cathedral had been installed. Today, the cathedral thrives as a place of worship and hospitality, welcoming over 700,000 people every year. Unusually, this example of Norman architecture has survived largely intact over the centuries, making it a valuable piece of history and of national architectural importance. Almost every other Norman construction has been either knocked down or modified beyond recognition and consequently Durham Cathedral and Durham Castle are amongst the finest surviving examples of Norman architecture in Europe. Between them, Durham University and Durham Cathedral house an array of rare and valuable manuscripts and other documents recording the history of the Diocese of Durham. Its historical and ecclesiastical relevance is more important that its architectural value. The shrines of St Cuthbert and the Venerable Bede are at the cathedral.

Saint Cuthbert, b. 635, d. 687

Cuthbert was a monk, bishop and hermit in places of worship around Northumbria. After he died pilgrims visiting his grave started reporting miracles. During the threat of various invasions, poor old Cuthbert's bones were carted around by some monks, who finally let them rest in Durham. Cuthbert remains the patron saint of Northern England.

Venerable Bede, b. 673, d. 735

Bede is generally regarded as the greatest of all the Anglo-Saxon scholars. He was a deacon and later a priest. He wrote around forty books during his lifetime on the themes of theology, history, nature, poetry and music. His most famous work is *Historia Ecclesiastica Gentis Anglorum*, translated as *The Ecclesiastical History of the English People*, which he finished in AD 731. It gives the background to the introduction of Christianity to England.

Did You Know?

According to the website durhamworldheritagesite.com, 'the Cathedral has been in continuous use since its original construction 900 years ago … It holds over 1,700 services a year, and costs £60,000 per week (that's about £6 per minute!) to maintain.'

Stokesay Castle

This castle is located 7 miles north-west of Ludlow, in Shropshire, and was built at the end of the thirteenth century by Laurence of Ludlow, a successful wool merchant and one of the richest men in England. Technically it is a fortified manor house rather than a castle. The building and land remained in the family of Laurence of Ludlow for more than 300 years. The Earls of Craven owned the building at several points and it survived a destruction order from Oliver Cromwell. It was lovingly repaired and restored by private owners from the mid-nineteenth century and opened to the paying public for the first time in 1908. The last descendant of private owners, Jewell Magnus-Allcroft, agreed to hand over the castle to English Heritage after years of expensive maintenance costs, and died in 1992. The shropshiretourism. co.uk website states, 'Stokesay's superb condition today is largely due to the care of its successive owners and the fact that it only changed hands five times in 700 years.'

Hardwick Hall, Derbyshire

Built between 1590 and 1597 by the super wealthy Bess of Hardwick, Countess of Shrewsbury and part of the family of the Dukes of Devonshire, this Elizabethan country house is a leading example of the 'prodigy' house. This was a house built to show wealth, power and connection. Prodigy houses were mainly built between 1570 and 1620. Elizabeth Talbot, otherwise known as Bess of Hardwick, was the richest woman in England after Queen Elizabeth I. She had married into money, more than once, and enjoyed displaying her riches and power. Hardwick Hall was a remarkable statement of her wealth; a demonstration of opulence, extravagance and Elizabethan success and confidence. Hardwick Hall shows a rising concern for comfort, a long way from the wealthy or titled who needed a moat or a portcullis for defence. This was a financially stable time and a peaceful one too. Landowners were reaping the rewards from rising prices of produce and many others benefitted from the expansion of overseas trade.

Hardwick Hall was probably designed by Robert Smythson and remains an historically significant piece of architecture influenced by Renaissance styles from Florence but with its own character reflected in the design as well. So many windows were included in the design at a time when glass was a luxury and a symbol of wealth. Elizabeth Goldring points out that Hardwick Hall is the earliest surviving example of an English house with loggias but no internal courtyard. Goldring also states that 'it was rather unusual that the hall, rather than running parallel to the long axis of the house, is instead placed at a right angle to it'. It was customary at the time for the main room to receive guests to be located on the first floor but Bess put hers on the second floor. This meant that guests could see an extra floor of ostentatious art, furniture and tapestries before greeting their host.

The Royal Observatory, London

The Royal Observatory was built during the reign of King Charles II in the 1600s and has been referred to as the 'home of time'. Positioned on a hill in Greenwich Park, overlooking the River Thames, it has played a major role in the history of astronomy, navigation, map making, timekeeping and scientists' first mapping of the seas and stars. The Observatory is used in navigation and shipping as the prime meridian, the exact line passing through from the North to South Pole. It divides the globe into the Eastern and Western Hemispheres. You can stand astride a long metal strip on the floor and be standing across two hemispheres. Nations across the world have used it as their standard for both mapping and timekeeping. Today, the Royal observatory holds a hyper accurate clock, the UK's largest refracting telescope and a 4.5-billion year-old asteroid. The Royal Observatory literally put England on the world map when it came to astronomy, maps, time and navigation. It is where the term Greenwich Mean Time comes from. The Royal Observatory's tradition of meridian astronomy enhanced the reputation of the nation and Empire when it became the location of the world's prime meridian. Knowledge and utility were all about international prestige, status and respect.

Caernarfon Castle

On the death of Henry III in 1272 his son Edward was on the Eighth Crusade. Edward hastily returned to London, determined to stamp his authority over the British Isles, and controlling Wales was an important part of this. Llywelyn ap Gruffudd, ruler of Gwynedd, refused to pay homage to King Edward I of England. The consequence was Edward's brutal conquest of Gwynedd. After he had defeated the Welsh leader, Edward built a ring of castles to enforce his rule. Wales was brought into the English legal and administrative framework. Caernarfon Castle has been called 'a muscular monster of a fortress' and is one of the most imposing and impressive castles, not just in Wales, but in the whole of Britain. King Edward I built Caernarfon Castle in the 1280s to show the Welsh that the English were dominant over them and that he was in charge. Edward carefully chose the

Caernarfon Castle. (© *Crown copyright (2016) Visit Wales*)

location to build an impressive castle; it had previously been the site of a Roman castle and a Norman motte and bailey castle, which no doubt had something to do with its coastal position. Caernarfon was part of a bigger castle-building programme and Edward spent the majority of the nation's income on this project.

The castle became a powerful symbol, a sign of absolute authority. Caernarfon became a seat of power and a show of might, something that Edward wanted everyone to see and understand. It was a heavily armed castle with portcullises, arrow loops, spy holes and murder holes. It was a castle to send an intimidating message to the locals, not to mess with their English king. Edward went one stage further and destroyed the Welsh settlement around the castle and replaced it with a new English incorporated town that eradicated generations of Welsh tradition and culture. In 1284, Edward's first son was born at the castle, and given the title Prince of Wales. In 1969 the current Prince of Wales, HRH Prince Charles's investiture also took place at Caernarfon.

The Globe Theatre

The idea of a purpose-built theatre to stage plays in was a relatively new idea in England (since their demise in Roman times). The first proper theatres were built during the reign of Elizabeth I (1558–1603). Until this time, performances usually took place at the local inn, in the courtyard or sometimes in the street. James Burbage built the first formal theatre, in London, in 1576. Soon after, other people constructed theatres, including The Rose (1587), The Globe (1599) and The Hope (1613).

The Globe was an impressive amphitheatre-type building, a theatre holding several thousand people. It also had a reputation for being used as a brothel and a gambling den at times. Old maps of London show what the exterior looked like but we can only use the inside of The Swan Theatre as a guide (they were very similar and drawings of The Swan still exist). It was built by the production company that William Shakespeare had shares in and proved to be very popular. In fact, there was serious competition between the different theatres in London. There would be many market stalls around the theatre selling a variety of products. The atmosphere drew in crowds from miles around, many of whom would not even be going to the theatre. Some were happy to purchase food from the numerous vendors and enjoy an almost carnival like atmosphere. The colour of the flag above The Globe would tell the crowds what type of play they were about to see; red for history, black for tragedy and white for comedy. The Globe's trumpeter would announce the impending start of the play and the crowds would make their way to the entrance, putting a penny into the box on the way in. It was a penny to stand in the 'pit' and enjoy the show from the ground. It cost a little more to separate yourself from the unwashed crowds (groundlings as they were known) and enjoy one of the seats elevated above the masses. It was an extra penny to go up one level and you had to put your money in the box. If you wanted to go ever even further up then you had to give another penny to the man holding a box. It was his job to collect the money for the better seats. All the box men gathered in a room to count the money and share it out. This room was called the box office. This is why today's theatre has a box office selling tickets.

Elizabeth I was fully aware of the propaganda power of the theatre, with its religious and political plays, but was not keen on imposing strict controls. Nevertheless, heated rows often broke out in the more contentious performances. Many plays were rude and bawdy, the audiences calling out and jeering throughout the performance, creating a rowdy atmosphere. This was not seen as rude, as it would be today, it was Elizabethan theatre culture. It was not unknown for gentlemen to relieve themselves in the pit because there was nowhere else to go. Add this stench to that of several thousand sweaty people (many did not wash regularly) and you can begin to appreciate the smell emanating from the pits. After the plays ended, the streets were a noisy place with bustling crowds, providing a breeding ground for petty crime, and indeed crime rates increased in these areas.

Ham House

This beautiful house and garden, near Richmond on the outskirts of London, is a fine example of seventeenth-century architecture. It was built in 1610 by William Murray and his daughter Elizabeth. Murray was an enterprising courtier and a favourite of King Charles I, probably because they were educated together and William was his whipping boy. A young prince could not be whipped by the teacher if he did something wrong, so another boy had to take the punishment for him. All princes had whipping boys and they were often handsomely rewarded. Their friendship developed during adulthood and in 1626 King Charles gave William a 999-year lease on Ham House and its estate. William lovingly restored and decorated the house and made a number of alterations. When many once-royal lavish residences were taken over by Oliver Cromwell, William's daughter Elizabeth pretended to be on the Lord Protector's side, all the time secretly staying in contact with the exiled prince on the Continent. Meanwhile, Ham House remained in Elizabeth's family for nearly 300 years until it passed to the National Trust in 1948. The lack of alterations and updates makes Ham House a reliable testimony to seventeenth-century architecture, decoration and taste.

Stonehenge

Stonehenge, a ring of prehistoric monumental standing stones and one of Britain's oldest monuments, lies 8 miles north of Salisbury in Wiltshire. It dates back 3,000 years. The famous stones came from the Preseli Hills in Wales, about 135 miles from Wiltshire, quite an engineering achievement thousands of years ago. Nobody is really sure what the site was used for, but suggestions have ranged from astronomy to sacrifice. Evidence from archaeologists indicates that it was used possibly as a burial place at some

(*Photo: Kirstin Pettet*)

point in its history. This book suggests that it was a primitive type of clock, rather like a sundial, using the sun to gauge the different times of the day. As a tourist you can get close to the stones at this World Heritage site (since 1986) but you can no longer walk around them.

Scarborough

This seaside town was close to Maureen's heart, for this is where she spent many family holidays as a child in the 1950s and 1960s and she had nothing but happy memories of the town. The old school seaside landladies are a special breed and known not just throughout the British Isles, but throughout the world too for their feisty and formidable natures. Don't cross them, unless of course you are of the fearless kind. The B&B boom occurred in the post-war years of the 1950s when few had cars and a week at the seaside was a real luxury. Families would pile on to trains, which in turn were packed to over-flowing, and set off on their annual break

This is as far as my mother got in her story before she died of cancer, so I will take up the reins here. I too spent some of my early childhood days in Scarborough, as did my parents, grandparents and even great-grandparents. Personally, I don't even think the resort has changed that much since the 1970s, certainly not in spirit. In England's North-East, Scarborough was considered the Caribbean, Venice, Cannes and Far East in its day, all rolled into one. In the years after the Second World War, you were quite someone to be able to afford a treat like this – a day or even a weekend at Scarborough. However, Scarborough remains a popular seaside resort despite the influx of cheap package holidays.

Whitby, Yorkshire

Not many towns have made the final edit of this book but Whitby had to be included because of its unique character, unpretentious setting and welcoming features. The small port survives on fishing and tourism for its income. The local population is just over 13,000. Its history goes back a long way: Roman mining, a seventh-century abbey and the arrival of the Vikings. The Georgians loved Whitby and thus several multi-storeyed boarding

(*Photo: Kirstin Pettet*)

houses opened to accommodate a new wave of visitors. The Georgian tourists liked it because of three chalybeate springs that appeared in the town and these were consequently in demand for their supposed medicinal qualities. The town's tourism trade continued to blossom after the railway was built in the late 1830s. It has always been a tricky place to reach, even with modern roads. Today, visitors benefit from the redeveloped harbour, shops and restaurants. Whitbyonline.co.uk states says that the town has 'an eclectic mix of picturesque fisherman's cottages, storied Georgian town houses, cobbled streets, nooks and snickets'. In the 1740s James Cook (later Captain Cook) made his sea-faring debut from Whitby.

The Dingle, Shrewsbury

In the heart of Shrewsbury's Quarry Park is a large, sunken floral delight, set in landscaped grounds and surrounded by high hedges. Winding, descending paths lead you to a lake surrounded by overhanging trees and shrubs, as well as an open area displaying a visual feast of thousands of flowers, surrounded by benches. Spring is probably the best time to visit the Dingle, with the polyanthus, myosotis, tulips, daffodils and hyacinths taking centre stage. The statue of Sabrina, the water nymph of the River Severn, stands proudly amongst the flowerbeds admiring their beauty, as well as the perfectly trimmed lawns, trees, fountains and wildlife. This former stone quarry was rescued and renovated by the late Victorians, funded by  the Shropshire Horticultural Society and opened to the public in 1879. The world famous gardener Percy Thrower was appointed Park Superintendent in 1946, and transformed it into what it is today.

The Dingle, Shrewsbury, past and present. (*Images supplied by David Benson*)

Chapter 7

The English Language

English is a remarkable, changeable, flexible and even confusing language. However, it is one of the most influential and recognisable languages on the planet. History has played a part in its development, encouraging it to absorb the linguistic contributions of the Celts, Romans, Anglo-Saxons and Normans. It has welcomed words from Shakespeare and other literary greats before flourishing during the days of the Empire and Industrial Revolution, and even today's slang, technological influence and teen speak have added to its vocabulary. It has taken hundreds of years for this language to arrive at its current stage. Students only have to study Shakespeare or Chaucer to find the evidence that it has changed so much. The English language has not stopped developing and new words appear in the dictionary every year. Latin still plays a major part in the English language, not only contributing to its current make-up directly or indirectly, but also as the language of science and law. English is related to German, Dutch, Scandinavian languages and many others, through trade, war, invasion and friendship.

Latin Phrases Commonly Used in the English Language

Latin	English Meaning
Carpe diem	Seize the day.
Vice versa	With positions turned.
Ad captandum	An argument that appeals to the mob, rather than reason.
Bona fide	Good faith (trustworthy).
Verbatim	Word for word.
Absolutum dominium	Total power or sovereignty.
Per annum	Each year.
Quid pro quo	I give so that you may give/this for that.
Per se	By itself or in itself.
Habeas corpus	You should have the body. A legal term referring to a prisoner's right to challenge the legality of their detention.
Persona non grata	Unwanted or undesirable person.
Et cetera	And the rest … and so on …
Post scriptum (now shortened to PS)	After what is written.
Post mortem	After death.

The English language has also taken thousands of words from the Greek language. Some come from myths of gods and goddesses, especially from the stories taken from ancient Greece. Here is a very small sample of these terms, expressions and words that have added to the rich culture of the English language.

Greek Phrases and Words in the English Language

The Midas touch	To have good fortune in everything you do. This expression comes from the story of King Midas who was granted one wish and wanted everything he touched to turn to gold. In modern day parlance this refers to someone who succeeds in everything he or she does.
Chronology	The arrangement of events or dates in the order of their occurrence, this word is taken from Cronos, the ancient Greek god of time.
Phobia	This word comes from Phobos, the son of the Greek god Ares. The literal meaning of Phobos is 'fear' or 'terror'.
Echo	This word has its roots in ancient Greece, named after a mythical mountain nymph who talked excessively.
Achilles heel	This refers to a weakness or flaw, and is derived from Achilles, the Greek hero of the Trojan War who was dipped in the River Styx to make him immortal, but being held by his heels this part remained vulnerable.
Hypnosis	Meaning 'sleep-like state', this comes from the god of sleep who was called Hypnos.
Fortune	Meaning good luck, taken from the Greek goddess of luck, Fortuna.
To harp (on)	This means to keep complaining, from the Greek mythological bird with the head of a beautiful woman. The 'harpies' were seen as cruel and mean.

The English language contains some of the most interesting words in the world.

Fascinating English Words

Unusual English Word	Meaning
Discombobulating	Confusing the issue or matter.
Hippopotomonstrosesquippedaliophobia	Fear of long words.
Extemporaneous	To perform without preparation.
Mellifluous	A sweet, polite, educated (usually female) tone.
Pernickety	Over precise.
Floccinaucinihilipilifiaction	To reduce something to nothing.

Further Peculiarities of the English Language

In Britain we speak English – and many variations of it too. There are accents from around Great Britain where the same words are spoken in a variety of ways, where modulation and intonation differs, as does accentuations. There are dialects where a regional variation of the language means that different words are used to the standard English word, with quite often a variation in the grammatical usage too. Now, as if that isn't confusing enough there is also added into the mix the slang versions of some words. Slang is a very casual approach to a language and most languages have a series of slang words in everyday use. These words seem to be class, profession, society or club driven, which makes it confusing for even natives of the original language and therefore virtually impossible for those not familiar with the standard language. Take English, for example, which is the native language of both North America and Great Britain, and you will find that there are vast differences in the slang used. Here you will find just a few English slang words – with just the occasional reference to their American counterpart. Slang often has a short shelf life too and words change, disappear or are added each year as society moves on. Suddenly all those Latin lessons at school now seem quite straightforward and logical and the little ditty we used to sing before the lesson even funnier:

> Latin is a language
> As dead as dead can be;
> Once it killed the Romans
> And now it's killing me!

Common English Slang and Swear Words

Word/Phrase	Meaning
Arse	This is used when referring to the anatomical 'bottom' of a person. The American equivalent is 'ass', which in the UK means a donkey.
Arse about face	Doing something back to front.
Au fait	A French expression which has become part of the English language and means to be familiar with something.
Bees knees	Words to use when you think something is fabulous!
Bladdered	A word often used by the youth of the day to describe someone who is in a drunken state.
Budge up	If you want to sit next to someone and you feel that they are taking up too much space, you might ask them to 'budge up' – move up to make more space for you.
Chat-up	It is when you speak to someone of the opposite sex in a flirty and complimentary way in order to attract their attention.
Cheesed off	This is a polite way of saying 'fed up'.
Codswallup	Someone might say this to you when they think that you are talking a lot of rubbish.
Diddle	If you 'diddle' someone, then you are trying to rip them off.
Dishy	A word used to describe someone who is attractive.
Doddle	A word used to describe an easy task.
Easy peasy	Children love this one – a longer way of saying something is easy.
Faff	To faff about is to dither and dally, to procrastinate or to waste time doing absolutely nothing at all.
Fancy	This word is often used in relation to the opposite sex. When we say we 'fancy' someone then we are actually saying that we like them a lot and want to get to know them better.
Fiddlesticks	Really well-mannered individuals often say this word instead of a swear word.
Get lost	A not very nice way of telling someone who is generally irritating you to go away.
Give us a bell	Despite the use of the word 'us', this phrase means asking someone to telephone you sometime.
Grub	An alternative for the term food.

Word/Phrase	Meaning
Hanky-panky	An old fashioned way of saying someone is getting 'up to no good' with a member of the opposite sex.
At Her Majesty's pleasure	In England this is a polite way of saying you are being kept in prison.
Horses for courses	This means that what suits one person won't necessarily suit another.
Jammy	Means lucky.
Khazi	An alternative word for toilet.
Kip	Someone who is going to have a kip is actually going to have a short nap.
Knock-off	If you are told that something is knock-off it means that it is stolen.
Leg it	If you are told 'leg it', then you are being told to run away … quickly!
Lurgy	If you have the lurgy, then you are ill.
Morish	Also spelt 'moreish', this word is used when a single helping is simply not enough. You need more!
Mufti	This is an old army name for civvies, or civilian clothes. Children now have 'mufti' days at school when they don't have to wear their school uniform.
Mug	If someone is a bit of a mug, it means they are gullible.
Mush	Rhymes with 'push', slang word for your mouth as in 'shut your mush'.
Mutt's nuts	If something is described as being 'the Mutt's' then you'll know it is fantastic or excellent. 'The Mutt's' is short for 'The Mutt's nuts' which is clearly another way of saying the 'Dog's Bollocks'!
Naff	If something is naff, it is basically uncool. You could also use it to tell someone to naff off, which is a more polite way of telling them to get lost!
Nancy boy	If someone is being pathetic you would call them a nancy or a nancy boy. It is the opposite of being 'hard'. For example, in cold weather a nancy boy would dress up in a coat, hat, gloves and scarf and a hard guy would wear a t-shirt. It's also another word for a gay man, although deemed derogatory, offensive and inappropriate.

Word/Phrase	Meaning
Nark	If someone is in a nark, it means they are in a bad mood, or being grumpy. It's also the word for a spy or informant. For example, a copper's nark is someone who is a police informant – which an American might call a stoolie or stool-pigeon. The origin is from the Romany word 'nak', meaning 'nose'.
Narked	In the UK you would say that someone looked narked if you thought they were in a bad mood. In the US you might say that someone was pissed, which in the UK would mean they were drunk!
Nesh	This is an uncommon way of referring to someone being a bit of a wimp.
Nice one!	If someone does something particularly impressive you might say 'nice one!' to them. It is close to the Texan 'good job'.
Nick	To nick is to steal. If you nick something you might well get 'nicked'.
Nicked	Something that has been stolen has been nicked. Also, when a copper catches a burglar red-handed he might say, 'you've been nicked!'.
Nitwit	See 'twit'.
Nookie	Nookie is the same as 'hanky-panky'.
Nosh	You would refer to food as nosh or you might be going out for a good nosh-up, or meal! Either way, if someone has just cooked you some nosh you might want to call it something else as it is not the nicest word to describe it.
Not my cup of tea	This is a common saying that means something is not to your liking. For example, if someone asked you if you would like to go to an all-night rave, they would know exactly what you meant if you told them it was not exactly your cup of tea!
Nowt	This is Yorkshire for nothing. Similarly 'owt' is Yorkshire for anything. Hence the expression, 'you don't get owt for nowt', which can be roughly translated as 'you never get anything for nothing', or 'there's no such thing as a free lunch'.
Nut	To nut someone is to headbutt them.
Off colour	If someone said you were off colour they would mean that you looked pale and ill!
Off your trolley	If someone tells you that you're off your trolley, it means you have gone raving bonkers, crazy, mad!

Word/Phrase	Meaning
On about	What are you on about? That's something you may well hear when visiting the UK. It means what are you talking about?
On the job	If you are on the job, it could mean that you are hard at work, or having sex. Usually the context helps you decide which it is!
On the piss	If you are out on the piss, it means you are out to get drunk, or to 'get pissed'.
On your bike	A very polite way of telling someone to get lost.
One-off	A one-off is a special or one-time event that is never to be repeated, such as writing this book!
Owt	This is Yorkshire for 'anything'. See 'nowt'.
Pants	This is quite a new expression of uncertain origin, but it is quite trendy now to say that something that is rubbish is 'pants'. For instance, you could say the last episode of a TV show was 'total pants'.
Parky	Either short for Michael Parkinson, a famous chat-show host, or more likely a word to describe the weather as being rather cold!
Pass	This means I don't know and comes from the old TV show *Mastermind*, where contestants were made to say 'pass' if they did not know the answer to the question.
Pavement pizza	This is a descriptive way of saying vomit, often found outside Indian restaurants early on a Sunday morning.
Peanuts	The full expression is that if you pay peanuts, you get monkeys. It is a fairly derogatory way of saying that you don't need to be bright to do manual labour and it doesn't pay well. Typically these days peanuts means something is cheap. For example, Brits would say the petrol in the US is peanuts or costs peanuts – compared with UK prices it is!
Pear-shaped	If something has gone pear-shaped it means it has become a disaster, for example, a dinner party or arranging a meeting.
Piece of cake	It means it's easy!
Pinch	This means to steal something. Though when you say 'steal' it is a bit more serious than pinch. A kid might pinch a cake from the kitchen. A thief would steal something during a burglary.
Pip pip	An out-dated expression meaning goodbye. Not used any more.
Piss poor	If something is described as being 'piss poor' it means it is an extremely poor attempt at something.

Word/Phrase	Meaning
A piss-up	This is a drinking session or a visit to the local pub. There is an English expression to describe someone as disorganised which says that he/she could not organise a piss-up in a brewery!
Pissed	This is a great one for misunderstanding. Most people go to the pub to get pissed. In fact the object of a stag night is to get as pissed as possible. Getting pissed means getting drunk. It does not mean getting angry; that is American, which in Britain would be 'getting pissed off'!
Plastered	Another word for loaded. In other words you have had rather too much to drink down your local. It has nothing to do with being covered with plaster, though anything is possible when you are plastered.
Porkies	More Cockney rhyming slang, short for 'porky pies', meaning 'pork pies' which rhymes with 'lies'. My mum always used to tell me I was telling porkies – and she was right!
Porridge	Doing porridge means to serve time in prison. There was also a comedy TV series called *Porridge* about a prisoner and starring Ronnie Barker of *The Two Ronnies* fame.
Posh	Roughly translates as high class. It comes from the cabins used by the upper class on early voyages from England to India. The coolest (and most expensive cabins) were port side on the way out and starboard on the way home.
Potty	This isn't just the thing you sit a toddler on – if you are potty it means you are a little crazy, a bit of a loony, one card short of a full deck.
Potty mouth	Refers to someone who swears a lot.
Pound sign	Ever wondered why Brits flounder when voicemail messages say to press the pound sign? What on earth is the British currency doing on a phone anyway? Well, it isn't. To a Brit, the pound sign is the wiggly thing used officially to denote the UK pound (or 'quid').
Prat	Yet another mildly insulting name for someone. In fact, this one is a bit ruder than 'pillock' so you probably wouldn't say it in front of grandma.
PTO	This is the acronym for 'please turn over'. You will see it on forms in the UK where you would see the single word in the US.
Puff	If a Brit starts giggling in an American drugstore, it may be because they have just found a box of 'Puffs'. To some Brits a 'puff' is another word for a fart, and stems from the cockney rhyming slang to 'puff a dart'.

Word/Phrase	Meaning
Pukka	This term has been revived recently by the TV chef Jamie Oliver. It means super or smashing, which of course is how he describes all his food.
Pull	It means looking for 'birds'. Of course, it works the other way round too and ladies may also be on the pull, though probably a bit more subtly than the chaps.
Pussy	This is what Brits call their cat, as in 'pussy cat' or in the fairytale *Puss in Boots*.
Put a sock in it	This is one way of telling someone to shut up. Clearly the sock needs to be put in their loud mouth!
Put paid to	This is an expression that means to put an end to something. For example, you could say that rain put paid to the cricket match, meaning it stopped play.
Queer	Apart from the obvious gay link, this word was once used a lot to mean someone looked ill. As in 'You look queer'. Of course, you might not say that these days in case you get either picked up or thumped!
Quid	A pound in money is called a quid. It is the equivalent to the buck or clam in America. A five-pound note is called a fiver and a ten-pound note is called a tenner.
Quite	When used alone, this word means the same as absolutely!
Rat arsed	Yet another term for drunk, 'sloshed' or 'plastered'. You might say loaded. In the UK, *Loaded* is a men's magazine that covers sex and football.
Read	If someone asks you what you read at university, they mean what subject did you study.
Really	This is one of those words where Americans say almost the same thing as the Brits, but just cannot be bothered to finish it off! The word is 'really', not real.
Redundancy	If you are made redundant it means you are laid off.
Reverse the charges	When you want to ring someone up and you have no money you can call the operator and ask to reverse the charges in the UK. In the US they would 'call collect'.
Right	I'm feeling 'right' knackered, meaning you are feeling very tired.
Ring	You would ring someone on the phone not call them, in the UK. I asked someone in an American shop to ring me up and he dragged me to the till and pulled my head across the scanner!

Word/Phrase	Meaning
Roger	Same kind of problem that Randy has here, except we have people called Roger and no Randys. You will see a strange smile on the face of a Brit every time 'Roger the Rabbit' is mentioned! To roger means to have your wicked way with a lady; the *Oxford English Dictionary* says to copulate and the slang word is 'screw'.
Round	When you hear the words 'your round' in the pub, it means it is your turn to buy the drinks for everyone in the group – nothing to do with the size of your tummy! Since beers are more and more expensive these days, the art of buying the rounds has developed into ensuring you buy the first one before everyone has arrived, without being obvious!
Row	Rhyming with 'cow', this means an argument. You might hear your mum having a row with your dad, or your neighbours might be rowing so loud you can hear them!
Rubbish	The stuff we put in the bin. Trash or garbage to an American. You might also accuse someone of talking rubbish.
Rugger	This is short for 'rugby'. It is a contact sport similar to American football but played in muddy fields during winter and rain. Not only that, but the players wear almost no protection!
Rumpy-pumpy	Another word for hanky-panky or a bit of nookie! Something two consenting adults get up to in private!
Sack/sacked	If someone gets the sack it means they are fired. Then they have been sacked.
Sad	This is a common word, with the same meaning as 'naff'. Used in expressions like 'you sad b***ard'.
Scrummy	This is a word that would most likely be used to describe some food that was particularly good (and probably sweet and fattening).
Scrumping	To go stealing, usually apples from someone else's trees!
Send-up	To send someone up is to make fun of them. Or if something is described as being a send-up it is equivalent to the American take-off. Like Robin Williams did a take-off on the British accent – quite well actually!
Shag	Same as 'bonk' but slightly less polite. At parties in the 70s the look of surprise on the Englishman's face when an American girl asked him if he would like to shag was amusing. Best way to get a Brit to dance! You can even go to shagging classes!
Shagged	Past tense of 'shag', but also see 'knackered'.

Word/Phrase	Meaning
Shambles	If something is a shambles it is chaotic or a real mess. It's also a very old name for a slaughterhouse. So if you ever visit The Shambles in York, then the name does not refer to the somewhat shambolic nature of the buildings but is a reference to the site it's built on – an old slaughterhouse!
Shambolic	In a state of chaos. Generally heard on the news when the government is being discussed!
Shirty	'Don't get shirty with me young man' was the sort of thing your dad would say to you when you were little, meaning you were getting bad tempered.
Shite	This is just another way of saying shit. It is useful for times when you don't want to be overly rude as it doesn't sound quite as bad!
Shitfaced	If you hear someone saying that they got totally shitfaced it means they were out on the town and got steaming drunk. Normally attributed to stag nights or other silly events.
Shufti	Pronounced 'shooftee', this means to take a look at something, to 'take a butchers'! It's an old Arabic word, picked up by British soldiers in North Africa during the Second World War.
Sixes and sevens	If something is all at sixes and sevens then it is in a mess, topsy turvy or somewhat haywire!
Skew-whiff	This is what you would call crooked. Like when you put a shelf up and it isn't straight but all skew-whiff.
Skive	To skive is to evade something. Kids might skive off school to avoid doing maths. They are always caught, of course, presumably because the teachers used to do the same when they were 14!
Slag	To slag someone off, is to bad mouth them in a nasty way, usually to their face.
Slapper	A slapper is a female who is a bit loose. A bit like a 'slag' or a 'tart'. It translates as 'tramp' in American.
Slash	Something a 'lager lout' might be seen doing in the street after his curry – 'having a slash'. Other expressions used to describe this bodily function include 'siphon the python', 'shake the snake', 'wee', 'pee', piss, 'piddle' and 'having a jimmy'.
Sloshed	Yet another way to describe being drunk. Clearly a lot of ways to describe this are required since getting 'plastered' is a national pastime.

Word/Phrase	Meaning
Smarmy	Another word for a smoothy, someone who has a way with the ladies, for example. Usually coupled with 'git' – as in 'what a smarmy git'. Not meant to be a nice expression, of course.
Smart	When Brits say someone is smart, they are talking about the way they are dressed – you might say they look sharp. When Americans say someone is smart they are talking about how intelligent or clever someone is.
Smashing	If something is smashing, it means it is terrific.
Smeg	This is a rather disgusting word, popularised by the TV show *Red Dwarf*. Short for 'smegma', the dictionary definition says it is a 'sebaceous secretion from under the foreskin'. Now you know why it has taken me three years to add it in here – not nice! Rather worryingly smeg is also the name of a company that makes domestic appliances!
Snap	This is a card game where the players turn cards at the same time and shout 'snap' when they match. People also say 'snap' when something someone else says has happened to them too. For example, when I told somebody that my wallet was stolen on holiday, they said 'snap', meaning the same thing had happened to them!
Snog	If you are out on the pull you will know you are succeeding if you end up snogging someone of the opposite sex (or same sex for that matter!). Americans would probably refer to it as 'making out', or serious kissing!
Snookered	If you are snookered it means you are up the famous creek without a paddle. It comes from the game of snooker where you are unable to hit the ball because the shot is blocked by your opponent's ball.
Sod	This word has many uses. 'Oh Sod!' or 'Sod it!' can be used if something has gone wrong and you don't want to swear too badly in front of the children. If someone is a sod or an 'old sod' then it means they are a bit of a bastard or an old git. 'Sod off' is like saying 'piss off' or 'get lost' and 'sod you' means something like 'f*** off'. It also means a chunk of lawn of course. You can usually tell the difference!
Sod all	If you are a waiter in the US and you serve a family of Brits, the tip is likely to be sod all or, as you would call it, nothing. Because Brits are generally poor tippers.
Sod's law	This is another name for Murphy's law – whatever can go wrong, will go wrong.

Word/Phrase	Meaning
Sorted	When you have fixed a problem and someone asks how it is going you might say 'sorted'. It's also popular these days to say 'get it sorted' when you are telling someone to get on with the job.
Spend a penny	To spend a penny is to go to the bathroom. It is a very old-fashioned expression that is still in use today. It comes from the fact that in public toilets you used to operate the door by inserting an old penny.
Splash out	If you splash out on something it means you throw your senses out the window, get out your credit card and spend far too much money. You might splash out on a new car or even on a good meal.
Squidgy	A chocolate cream cake would be squidgy. It means to be soft and, well, squidgy!
Squiffy	This means you are feeling a little drunk. Some people also use it to mean that something has gone wrong.
Starkers	Avoid being seen starkers when visiting England. It means stark naked.
Stiffy	Yet another word for erection.
Stone the crows	This is an old expression with the same meaning as 'cor blimey'.
Stonker	This means something is huge. Looking at a large burger, you might say 'blimey, what a stonker'. It is also used to refer to an erection! Clearly English modesty is a myth!
Strop	If someone is sulking or being particularly miserable you would say they are being stroppy or that they have a strop on. I heard an old man on the train tell his wife to stop being a stroppy cow.
Stuff	This is slang for saying forget about something because you do not care. For example, stuff the rain, let's go for a walk. Stuff you, him, her is suggesting one does not care about what someone does or thinks.
Suss	If you heard someone saying they had you sussed they would mean that they had you figured out! If you were going to suss out something it would mean the same thing.
Sweet fanny adams	This means nothing or 'sod all'. It is a substitute for 'sweet f*** all'. It is also shortened further to 'sweet FA'.
Swotting	Swotting means to study hard, the same as 'cram' does. Before exams you swot, not that it makes any difference to some of us. If you swotted all the time, you would be called a swot – which is not a term of endearment!

Word/Phrase	Meaning
Ta	We said 'ta' as kids for years before we even knew it was short for thanks.
Table	To Brits a motion is tabled when it is brought to the table, or suggested for consideration. Conversely, Americans table a motion when it is left for a later date.
Taking the biscuit	If something really takes the biscuit, it means it out-does everything else and cannot be bettered. In some places in the US they said 'takes the cake'.
Taking the mickey	See 'taking the piss'. Variations include 'taking the mick' and 'taking the Michael'.
Taking the piss	One of the things Americans find hardest about the Brits is their sense of humour. It is obviously different and is mainly based on irony, sarcasm and an in-built desire to 'take the piss'. This has nothing to do with urine, but simply means making fun of someone.
Talent	Talent is the same as 'totty'. Checking out the talent means looking for the sexy young girls (or boys).
Tara	This is another word for 'cheerio' or goodbye. Cilla Black, the late Scouse TV presenter, probably did most to promote the use of this word as she said it all the time on her programmes.
Throw a spanner in the works	This is an expression that means to wreck something.
Tickety-boo	If something is going well with no problems it is tickety-boo.
Tidy	Apart from the obvious meaning of neat, tidy also means that a woman is a looker, attractive or sexy.
To	Brits go to school from ages 5 to 18. Americans go to school from ages 5 thru 18. Brits don't say thru in that context at all. If we did, though, we would say 'through'!
Todger	As if there aren't enough of them already, this is yet another word for your 'willy', or penis.
Toodle pip	This is an old expression meaning goodbye. However, it is only heard when Americans are doing impressions of Brits as it has fallen into disuse, along with steam trains and gas lights.
Tool	Yet another word for your 'willy', or penis. You'd think we were obsessed!
Tosser	This is another word for 'wanker' and has exactly the same meaning and shares the same hand signal.

Word/Phrase	Meaning
Totty	If a chap is out looking for totty, he is looking for a nice girl to chat up. There is an Italian football player called Totti, which is pronounced the same. It's really funny hearing the commentators when he gets the ball saying 'it's Totty for Italy' – it sounds like some beautiful Italian girls have invaded the pitch.
TTFN	Short for 'ta ta for now', which in turn means goodbye.
Twee	Twee is a word you would generally hear older people say. It means dainty or quaint. A bit like the way Americans think of England.
Twit	You twit! Not so rude as calling someone an idiot but it amounts to the same thing. Remember Monty Python's 'Twit of the Year' competition? Other versions include 'nitwit'. Do not confuse this with the word 'twat' which is considered rather rude and is quite an insult!
Two-finger salute	When you see a Brit stick up two fingers at you in a V shape, he may be ordering two of something (if his palms are toward you). The other way around and it's an insult along the lines of the American one-finger salute. Which, by the way, is very popular with Brits now too!
U	A letter used far more in English. It is in words like colour, favour and labour.
Uni	Short for university, Brits would say they went to uni, whilst Americans would say they went to school. School in Britain is just for children.
Wacky backy	This is the stuff in a joint, otherwise known as pot or marijuana!
Waffle	To waffle means to talk on and on about nothing. It is not just something you eat. Americans often think that Brits waffle on about the weather.
Wangle	Some people have all the luck. Some people can wangle anything – upgrades on planes, better rooms in hotels.
Watcha	Simply means Hi. Also short for 'what do you' as in 'watcha think of that?'
Waz	On average, it seems that for every pint of lager you need to go for a waz twice! A complete waste of time in a serious drinking session. It means wee or pee.
Well	Well can be used to accentuate other words. For example, someone might be 'well hard' meaning he is a real man, as opposed to just 'hard'. Something really good might be 'well good'. Or if you were really, really pleased with something you might be 'well chuffed'. Grammatically it's appalling but people say it anyway.

Word/Phrase	Meaning
Welly	If you 'give it welly', it means you are trying harder or giving it the boot. An example would be when accelerating away from lights, you would give it welly to beat the guy in the Mustang convertible in the lane next to you. Welly is also short for 'wellington boots', which are similar to American galoshes.
Whinge	Whingers are not popular in any circumstance. To whinge is to whine. We all know someone who likes to whinge about everything.
Willy	Another word for penis. It is the word many young boys are taught as it is a nicer word than most of the alternatives. Some people also use it for girls as there are no nice alternatives. Hence 'woman's willy'. Also used by grown-ups who don't wish to offend (this word is safe to use with elderly grandparents).
Wind-up	This has a couple of meanings. If something you do is a 'wind-up' it means you are making fun of someone. However, if you are 'wound up' it means you are annoyed.
Wobbler	To 'throw a wobbly' or to 'throw a wobbler' means to have a tantrum. Normally happens when you tell your children they can't have an ice cream or that it's time for bed.
Wonky	If something is shaky or unstable you might say it is wonky. For example, I changed my chair in a restaurant recently because I had a wonky one.
Write to	When visiting the US one can't help noticing that Americans write each other – they don't 'write to' each other. In the UK it would be grammatically incorrect to say 'write me' and you would be made to write it out 100 times until you got it right.
Yakking	This means talking incessantly.
Yonks	'Blimey, I haven't heard from you for yonks'. If you heard someone say that it would mean that they had not seen you for ages!
Zed	The last letter of the alphabet. Brits hate saying 'zee' and only relent with names such as ZZ Top (Zed Zed Top does sound a bit stupid!).
Zip it!	A cheeky way of saying shut up! 'Belt up' is another way, considered a little ruder. It all depends how you say it as well!
Zonked	If someone is zonked or 'zonked out' it means they are totally 'knackered' or you might say exhausted. When a baby has drunk so much milk, his eyes roll into the back of his head, it would be fair to say he is zonked!

Speaking English

There is a saying, in fact there is a line from a song, and it goes: 'Mad dogs and Englishmen go out in the midday sun.' And maybe it was when out in the midday sun that one of these English men created our language, because there is nothing logical or sane about it, that's for sure! British people get confused at times, so exactly what hope do the non-British have in trying to understand it? None at all, that's what!

As if the English language isn't difficult enough already, there are further differences, for example, there are regional accents. This is the way in which words are pronounced, which in turn indicates the place from which the speaker originates, or indeed even his social background. Then there are dialects, which are regional differences of the English language that have their own variations in vocabulary, even their own, and often peculiar, use of grammar and their own pronunciation. In other words, what may be correct in one area of the British Isles could easily be incorrect, or even unheard of, just 50 miles along the coast. At times even the British find it difficult to understand each other, so visitors here must be frequently at a complete loss (for words, as the saying goes!).

Take a Look at These

Once you have learned the meaning of a word and how to spell it, then you would think that that was the end of it wouldn't you? Not so, because two words can be spelt exactly the same, but because they are pronounced differently they then have entirely different meanings, or spelled slightly differently but be pronounced in the same way and yet have different meanings. You only have to take a look at these examples below to see just how ridiculous and confusing the English language can be.

1. The local council tip was so full of **refuse** that the foreman had to **refuse** to allow more tipping that day.
2. The nurse **wound** the bandage around the **wound**.
3. Sally told Jack to wait to **present** the **present** to his boss.
4. If you **break** the **brake** you will have an accident.
5. If you **ring** me on Wednesday I'll be able to tell you whether your **ring** has arrived.

6. I couldn't help but shed a **tear** when I saw the **tear** in my wedding dress.
7. The cupboard was so **close** to the door that she was unable to **close** it.
8. There was a **row** between the friends on just how to **row** the boat.
9. The hero **caught** the boy who jumped from the house when it **caught** fire.
10. The overweight traveller decided to **desert** her **dessert** in the **desert**!
11. I **intimated** to my most **intimate** friend that it was time she grew up.
12. It's a **great** fire **grate** in that large house.

And Where is the Logic in This?

- Why do our noses run AND our feet smell?
- One mouse, two mice; one house, two houses or should that be 'hice'?
- How can a slim chance and a fat chance be the same thing and yet a wise man and a wise guy are opposites?
- If one hanky turns into two hankies, why does one monkey become two monkeys and not monkies?
- If 'I am' is the shortest sentence in the English language, why some would say that 'I do' is the longest sentence?
- Why do we recite at a play and play at a recital?

Changes in Meaning

Once you have learned an English word there is no guarantee that its meaning will remain the same. History has taught us that; just take a look at a few of the recent changes we have recently witnessed. It was not long ago that:

- A **gay** man was quite simply a happy little soul.
- **Crumpets** were something we had for tea, and that's all.
- A **Big Mac** was not to be eaten, for it was a very large raincoat to keep us dry in the dreadful British weather.
- We mowed the **grass**, not smoked it, just as a **joint** was something we roasted on a Sunday and didn't smoke.
- **Coke** was something to be found in a coalhouse.
- Mention the word **stud** now and a man would take it as a compliment, but sixty years ago and he would assume you were talking about the stud that fastened his collar to his shirt!

- Once a **fit** man was a healthy man, now a fit man is good looking … and not necessarily healthy either!
- **Going all the way** used to mean that you intended to stay on the bus until it reached the terminus; it then came to mean having full sex.
- Years ago a **wicked** person was to be feared, whereas now they are to be admired!
- **Chip** was a word used to describe a fried potato or a piece of wood and computers never entered one's head
- **Hardware** was quite simply nuts and bolts and you know what, no one had ever heard of **software**!
- **Pot** was something used to cook in.
- The word **aids** was used to describe a beauty treatment and not an illness.

Dialects

There are regional differences in dialects too, differences that confuse us all, whilst at the same time enthusing us with their rich and colourful language often only known to the true natives of these regions. For example, there follows a few Yorkshire words so when you visit this particular county you might just understand what they're saying.

Common Yorkshire Words and Phrases

Yorkshire Term	Meaning
Allus	Always
Any road	Is the Yorkshire way of saying 'anyway'
Aye	Yes
Bad 'un	No good
Bairn	Affectionate name for a small child
Barmy	Mad or crazy
Beck	A small river or stream
Belt up	Shut up
Blue murder	Big trouble
Bracken	Ferns
Champion	Excellent
Dollop	Lump or piece of something
Gumption	Common sense
Jiggered	Tired, exhausted
Kack-handed	Clumsy
Narky	Moody, sulky, stroppy
Nouse	Sense
Nowt	Nothing
Pell	Splinter
Sludge	Mud
Sup up	Drink up
Tallyman	Door to door collector of money

Remember that a Yorkshire person rarely uses the definite article (the) and so commands like: 'Shut the window' become 'shut winder'. Note the 'er' ending to the word instead of the 'ow' ending too; add to this the fact that an aitch at the beginning of a word is virtually unheard of (and virtually un'eard of in the middle too!) and you soon realise it really is verging on another language and not just a dialect. Some examples would be:

- You fell in **beck**? There'll be **blue murder** when yer mother sees yer clothes; you've got **sludge** all over 'em. Why didn't you use some **gumption** and cross by bridge; is there **nowt** i' yer 'ead?

Translation: You fell in the stream? There will be a lot of trouble when your mother sees your clothes; you've got mud all over them. Why didn't you use some common sense and cross by the bridge; is there nothing in your head?

- Put wood in 'ole.

Translation: Close the door.

Another much-loved dialect is Cockney rhyming slang which is admired and appreciated (although not necessarily understood!) throughout the world. True Cockneys must, it is said, be born within the sound of Bow Bells (St Mary-le-Bow Church), and if you saunter around that area itself you can almost guarantee you will hear this dialect, for Cockney rhyming slang is very much a living language. The cabbies will often chat to you using a smattering of Cockney and if you were ever to find yourself on a film set in London then you would hear the crew shouting instructions to each other in this colourful tongue; this can prove very confusing for any of the big American stars who might be filming here though!

Cockney Rhyming Slang

Cockney Phrase	Meaning
Adam and Eve	Believe
Apples and Pears	Stairs
Barnaby Rudge	Judge
Barnet Fair	Hair
Bees and honey	Money
Bo-Peep	Sleep
Cain and Able	Table
China plate	Mate (or friend)
Daisy roots	Boots
Dickory dock	Clock
Dicky bird	Word
Dog and bone	Phone
Dustbin lids	Kids
Friar Tuck	Luck
Garden gate	Magistrate
Ham and eggs	Legs
Hampstead Heath	Teeth
Harry Lime	Time
Harvey Nichol	Pickle
Heap of coke	Bloke
Jack Jones	Alone
Jack the Ripper	Kipper
Jam jar	Car
Jimmy Riddle	Piddle (have a 'wee' if you don't know what a piddle is!)
Jimmy Skinner	Dinner
Joanna	Piano
Khyber Pass	Arse

Cockney Phrase	Meaning
Lemon squash	Wash
Lilian Gish	Fish
Loaf of bread	Head
Mince pies	Eyes
North and south	Mouth
Oxo cube	The Tube
Plates of meat	Feet
Pork pie	Lie (sometimes called 'porkies')
Rocking horse	Sauce
Rosie Lee	Tea
Rub a dub dub	Pub
Saucepan lid	Kid (child)
Sexton Blake	Cake
Skin and blister	Sister
Tea leaf	Thief
Tit for tat	Hat (sometimes called a titfer)
Tom and Dick	Sick
Tommy Tucker	Supper
Trouble and strife	Wife
Two and eight	State
Uncle Ned	Bed
Whistle and flute	Suit

Be aware, though, that to understand this dialect not only do you have to know the relevant words but all the abbreviations too, for Cockneys often abbreviate their slang – just to make it even more difficult of course! Thus apples and pears meaning stairs is often cut down to just apples! Some examples would be:

- Get that featured extra on the **dog** and tell him that there's no budget for a **jam jar** and so he better get the **oxo** and tell him to keep his **minces** on the **dickory** this time too.

Translation: Get that featured extra on the 'phone and tell him that there's no budget for a car and so he better get the Tube and tell him to keep his eyes on the clock this time too.

- Fred and the **lids** are in a right **Harvey Nichol** since that **tea leaf** took all his **bees**.

Translation: Fred and the kids are in a right pickle since that thief took all his money.

Remember, as you wander around the UK, you may be an English-speaking native, but as you cross over from one county to another you will find that with many words that is where one word stops and another begins – for the same thing! One fine example is that good old English fayre – fish and chips; called the same thing all over the UK – right? Wrong!

The Origin or Meaning of Some British Traditions and Sayings

You have to feel sorry for anyone trying to learn the English language for, as we have seen, the spelling of some of the words just does not make any sense at all – not even to the British! But it doesn't end there, for in the English language there are sayings that have little to do with the actual words used. But if you think you could probably ask an Englishman to explain them to you, you need to think again because many of these sayings and traditions are so steeped in British heritage that many of the origins have been lost and most forgotten. But for amusement here are just a few that can be traced back in time.

The Bride's Bouquets
All brides like to carry a bouquet – and to be fair not just in Britain – and many like the place of the wedding ceremony adorned with floral

arrangements too. But have you ever wondered why, because there is a more practical reason than the aesthetics of the ceremony. In the days when it was normal for commoners to bathe a couple of times a year, the bride needed to disguise her intense and foul bodily odour to avoid putting off her husband. Therefore, she held a huge collection of beautiful smelling flowers. Naturally, people are a little cleaner today and fresher smelling but the tradition of the bride's bouquet has remained.

Dirt Poor

Even the poorest of society today have floor coverings, such as carpets, tiles, smart wooden floors etc. But in times gone by this was not the case and the poor could expect nothing but dirt on their floors, giving birth to the saying 'dirt poor'. The wealthy at this time enjoyed slate flooring, but this was not without its problems for during the bad winter months the floor became wet and slippery. Instead of drying it off with a rag, they, for some reason, covered the wet floor with straw, which was called thresh. As winter wore on, they added more and more thresh until there was so much that when the door was opened it would start slipping outside. It was at this point that a piece of wood was placed in front of the door to prevent this from happening, and so we have 'threshold' and 'carrying the bride over the threshold'. Probably a rag would have been so much easier!

Don't Throw the Baby Out with the Bath Water

Perish the thought; why would, or how could someone do that? Quite easily it would seem because this method of bathing, although dating back centuries, was still used in the 1950s when a bathroom in every house was not necessarily the 'norm'. In these cases a tub was filled with hot, clean water in which the man of the house took the first bath. He was followed by the other men and sons; next came the women, followed by the children and last of all the baby! By this time, as you can imagine, the water was anything but clean and in fact it was difficult to see anything, or anyone for that matter, submerged beneath. So, of course, a small baby could easily get lost in all the dirt and grime and so I suppose was in danger of being thrown out with the bath water. There were no plugs and drains which meant that the water was just literally thrown over any waste area. What this phrase actually means is don't make a mistake when trying to get rid of something bad.

Upper Crust

The British are renowned worldwide for being a society of classes – working class, middle class, upper class and so on, and there are sub-divisions within each of the classes just to confuse us it would seem! The words 'upper crust' fit into this structure and are derived from the old tradition of bread being divided according to social status. For example, the workers were given the burnt bottom of a loaf of bread, whereas the family was given the middle section and guests the top, or upper crust.

June Bride

Ever wondered why it is traditional to get married in June – although slowly we are losing the preference for this month. If you are about to arrange a June wedding yourself, you too might like to change the month when you know why it was so popular in the past! We take hot running water, and baths and showers in every home, for granted now, but it wasn't always like that. In fact centuries ago most people took their yearly bath in May and figured that in June they would still smell quite fresh and so that, along with warmer weather and churches, made it the ideal month in which to get married. Just in case they were starting to smell the bride carried a bouquet of flowers to hide her unsavoury body odour – hence the tradition of the 'bridal bouquet' too, as previously mentioned.

Kick the Bucket

This actually means to die and comes from a time when a criminal stood on a bucket whilst a rope was put around his neck; the bucket was then kicked from beneath him – the criminal was left hanging and so died.

Raining Cats and Dogs

In the Middle Ages England was mainly made up of a collection of farming communities. People worked the land, and the animals, for their survival. Having your animals stolen or perishing in the cold could be a costly business. Therefore, it was not unheard of for families to bring some of the animals inside, often up on the first floor away from the humans. Houses were not as sturdily built seven- or eight-hundred years ago, so when it rained some of the animals might fall through the interior roof, hence the saying 'it's raining cats and dogs'.

One for the Road

This saying dates back centuries and although today people are conscious of the perils of drink-driving, it is a saying still very much in use. So what's the origin of this dangerous saying? Years ago, when there were no motorised vehicles, prisoners in a certain part of London were taken to the gallows near Marble Arch which just happened to have a pub alongside it. The guard would then ask his prisoner if he would like one last drink. If he said yes, then that drink became known as 'one for the road'. If he declined the drink and stayed on the wagon transporting him to the gallows, then he was said to be 'on the wagon', which to this day means someone who has given up alcohol.

Saved by the Bell

Despite the marvels of modern medicine, there are still some people today who worry that no one will make sure that they are dead before they are taken off to the cemetery and as a consequence perhaps buried alive. Centuries ago they had a simple – if somewhat primitive – solution to this problem (and then it was a problem for often no one could be absolutely sure that a person was dead and frequently people were buried alive). So what did they do? Quite simply they tied a string onto the wrist of the corpse, which was then threaded through the coffin and up through the ground and tied to a bell. If a corpse woke up, he/she merely yanked their hand to ring the bell and alert the poor watchman detailed to sit by the grave overnight. This meant that a supposedly dead person was in effect 'saved by the bell'!

I'll be Mother

This is usually said when two or more people are faced with a teapot and several cups waiting to be filled. The person uttering these words is offering to pour out the tea for everyone present.

Not My Cup of Tea

This means that something is not to a someone's personal liking. Perhaps a friend models her new outfit for you and you might say, 'Well, it's not my cup of tea, but it does look good on you'. This means that although you personally don't like it and would never wear it, you have to admit that it does suit your friend.

Big Girl's Blouse

This cruel jibe or saying is one generally directed at someone who is considered to be weak or ineffectual in behaviour; as weak and as pathetic as a flimsy blouse on a little girl.

The Welsh Language

The Welsh language is very much a living language and often the first language spoken by many Welsh people, with businesses and schools all conducting their everyday lives in their native tongue of Welsh. Maureen's husband's family are all Welsh speaking and, unless being visited by an *English* person, family life is conducted entirely in Welsh. It was considered quite normal for her husband's little nephew of just 2 years old to speak to his grandparents in Welsh and his aunty, as the foreigner from England, in English – even the family dog was bi-lingual, accepting and obeying commands in both English and Welsh! It always fascinated Maureen that local shopkeepers always instinctively know that she was not Welsh speaking and so slipped in and out of the two different languages. Road signs are in the two languages as are menus and even lessons in schools. They are a clever lot, the Welsh, and yet don't seem to realise it, which makes it all the more endearing.

Despite being married to a Welshman for over thirty years, Maureen had only the vaguest grasp of the language, and found it far more difficult than French learned at school and even more difficult than Latin, which, along with Greek, was always a bit of a mystery! On the following page are a few basic phrases for you to try out – which will probably get you absolutely nowhere once you try to pronounce them, but you could always write them out and pass over the bit of paper!

Common Welsh Phrases

English	Welsh
Goodbye	Da boch chi
Goodnight	Nos da
Hello, how are you?	Helo, sut wyt ti?
How many?	Faint?
How much?	Faint?
How old are you?	Pa mor hen wyt ti?
My name is …	Fy enw i yw …
Please	Os gwelwch yn dda
I'm sorry	Maen ddrwg gen i
Thank you very much	Diolch yn fawr
Welcome	Croeso
What is your name?	Beth iw dy enw?
What time is it?	Faint o'r glochyw hi?
Where is …?	Ll mae …?
Will it rain?	Bydd yn bwrw glaw?
Would you like a cup of tea?	Fysa ti yn lecio paned o de?
Would you like something to eat?	Fysa ti yn lecio rhyw beth i fwyta?
Yes	Ia

The Welsh Alphabet

English	Welsh	Comment
A	A	
B	B	
C	C	
	ch	There is no ch in the English alphabet.
D	D	
	dd	There is no dd in the English alphabet.
E	E	
F	F	
	ff	There is no ff in the English alphabet.
G	G	
	NG	There is no NG in the English alphabet.
H	H	
I	I	
J	J	
K		There is no k in the Welsh alphabet.
L	L	
	LL	There is no LL in the English alphabet.
M	M	
N	N	
O	O	
P	P	
	PH	There is no PH in the English alphabet.
Q		There is no q in the Welsh alphabet.
R	R	
	RH	There is no RH in the English alphabet.
S	S	
T	T	
	th	There is no th in the English alphabet.
U	U	
V		There is no v in the Welsh alphabet.

English	Welsh	Comment
W	W	
X		There is no x in the Welsh alphabet.
Y	Y	
Z		There is no z in the Welsh alphabet.

Numbers in Welsh 'look', of course, exactly the same as in English. However, when written as a word they are entirely different, and if you could say them – would 'sound' – very different too.

Welsh Numbers

Number	Welsh Word
1	Un
2	Dau
3	Tri
4	Pedwar
5	Pump
6	Chwech
7	Saith
8	Wyth
9	Naw
10	Deg
11	Un deg un
12	Un deg dau
13	Un deg tri
14	Un deg pedwar
15	Un deg pump
16	Un deg chwech
17	Un deg saith
18	Un deg wyth
19	Un deg naw
20	Dau ddeg

Now for anyone not from Great Britain, worry not about learning this colourful language for it is almost impossible unless born into it, for you see Wales may be a part of Great Britain, but its language is another thing altogether.

The Best of English Writers

William Shakespeare

William Shakespeare has to be honoured with the title of one of Britain's most prolific, talented and well-known writers. He is often referred to as Britain's national poet. Shakespeare composed poems and sonnets, often for financial reasons when the plague closed London's theatres. Most schoolchildren have studied Shakespeare in some form, and most have struggled to get to grips with his tricky language. William Shakespeare was born in Stratford-upon-Avon in 1564 and gained a good reputation as an actor and writer, becoming well known in London. His acting company had interests in two theatres in the city: The Globe and The Blackfriars.

Some of Shakespeare's early work focused on histories and comedies. Some of these include *Henry VI*, *A Midsummer Night's Dream* and *The Merchant of Venice*. By the end of the sixteenth century and beginning of the seventeenth century, Shakespeare had become very well established as a poet and playwright. In the first few years of the seventeenth century Shakespeare penned some of his best tragedies, including *Hamlet*, *King Lear*, *Othello* and *Macbeth*. His plays include:

1. *Henry VI Part II* (1590–1).
2. *Henry VI Part III* (1590–1).
3. *Henry VI Part I* (1591–2).
4. *Richard III* (1592–3).
5. *The Comedy of Errors* (1592–3).
6. *Titus Andronicus* (1593–4).
7. *The Taming of the Shrew* (1593–4).
8. *The Two Gentlemen of Verona* (1594–5).
9. *Love's Labour's Lost* (1594–5).
10. *Romeo and Juliet* (1594–5).
11. *Richard II* (1595–6).
12. *A Midsummer Night's Dream* (1595–6).

13. *King John* (1596–7).
14. *The Merchant of Venice* (1596–7).
15. *Henry IV Part I* (1597–8).
16. *Henry IV Part II* (1597–8).
17. *Much Ado About Nothing* (1598–9).
18. *Henry V* (1598–9).
19. *Julius Caesar* (1599–1600).

Shakespeare's plays often have an underlying moral code, teaching the audience certain values. For example, *Macbeth* is about the dangers of over ambition, *Romeo and Juliet* is about the destructive power of hatred and *A Midsummer Night's Dream* warns about the complexity of love. Writers such as Claire Asquith (2005) claim that Shakespeare's works are littered with political codes and messages in support of suppressed Catholicism.

Mary Shelley – the Writer Who Gave us Frankenstein

Mary Wollstonecraft Godwin was born in England on 30 August 1797. Her mother, Mary Wollstonecraft, died when she was a baby and she was brought up by her father, William Godwin, and step-mother. She was homeschooled and mixed with literary greats of the time. At the age of 16 Mary ran off with a poet called Percy Bysshe Shelley, himself only 19 years old. The two of them later married and fled from England trying to escape the social disapproval of their scandalous relationship. The couple moved constantly throughout England, Switzerland and Italy.

Author Mary Shelley.

Mary conceived her magnum opus, *Frankenstein*, when she was only 19 at a house party with friends when they told each other made-up ghost stories. Mary's was about Frankenstein and her idea was born. It has often been referred to as the first great work of science fiction. After first putting pen to paper, it took Mary Shelly two years to complete the story. Mary Shelley's own story was rather sad, losing children, suffering a number of miscarriages and becoming a young widow. Mary died in 1851 at the age of 54 from a brain tumour. Shelley's biographer Suzanne Burdon acknowledged what she calls her intensity and enthusiasm for political and social reform and how it captured her imagination. Susan J. Wolfson and Ronald Levao refer to Frankenstein as 'the most enduring imaginative work of the Romantic era, even of the last 200 years'. In 1910, Thomas Edison Studios made the first film of *Frankenstein* (directed by J. Searle Dawley), followed in 1931 by James Whale's version starring Boris Karloff.

Mary's cottage on West Street, Marlow, England, still standing today and aptly renamed 'Shelley Cottage'. (*Photo: Kieran Hughes*)

Frankenstein is not the monster in the story but the name of the scientist who makes the monster and brings it to life. Therefore, *Frankenstein*'s subtitle *The Modern Prometheus* refers to the Greek mythological figure responsible for creating conflict between man and gods. He stole Zeus' fire, gave it to the people and was punished. He also made people out of clay and gave them life. Some of Mary Shelley's famous works include:

1. *Frankenstein; Or, The Modern Prometheus* (five different edns, 1818–31).
2. *Maurice; or, The Fisher's Cot* (1820).
3. *Valperga: Or, the Life and Adventures of Castruccio, Prince of Lucca* (1823).
4. *The Last Man* (1826).
5. *The Fortunes of Perkin Warbeck, A Romance* (1830).
6. 'Absence; "Ah! he is gone—and I alone!"' (poem) (1830).
7. 'A Night Scene; "I see thee not, my gentlest Isabel"' (poem) (1830).

8. *I Must Forget Thy Dark Eyes' Love-Fraught Gaze* (1832).
9. *Ode to Ignorance; 'Hail, Ignorance! majestic queen!'* (1834).
10. *Lodore* (1835).
11. *Falkner. A Novel* (1837).
12. 'How Like a Star You Rose Upon My Life' (poem) (1838).
13. *Mathilda* (1959, although written in 1818/19).

Charles Dickens, 1812–70

If this book is to detail the achievements of William Shakespeare, it must forward the literary clock to the nineteenth century to consider the quintessential Victorian author, entertainer, social commentator and historian Charles Dickens. He illustrated society's flaws of greed, selfishness and neglect. It was at a time when people were questioning their place in society, demanding a better deal, the vote, social fairness and asking whether the privileged classes should be in charge considering their incompetence and behaviour. Born in 1812 in Portsmouth, Dickens used the poverty and challenges of his childhood as motivation for some of his works. Dickens always had something to say through his fiction, whether it be a comment on factory conditions (something he'd endured as a child) the Poor Law Amendment Act (1834) or even speaking out against slavery. Dickens' biographer in the *Oxford Dictionary of National Biography*, Michael Slater, states that *David Copperfield* received 'considerable critical acclaim', thus widely considered to be his greatest piece of work. Perhaps thought of as the public's best-loved novel, Dickens himself referred to it as his 'favourite child'. In the book he called on his own life experiences and that of his family. Some of Dickens' works include:

1. *The Pickwick Papers* (1836).
2. *Oliver Twist* (1837).
3. *Nicholas Nickleby* (1838).
4. *A Christmas Carol* (1843).
5. *The Haunted Man* (1848).
6. *The Old Curiosity Shop* (1840).
7. *Barnaby Rudge* (1841).
8. *Martin Chuzzlewit* (1843).

9. *The Poor Relation's Story* (1852).
10. *Dombey and Son* (1846).
11. *David Copperfield* (1849).
12. *Bleak House* (1852).
13. *Pictures From Italy* (1846).
14. *Hard Times* (1854).
15. *Little Dorrit* (1855).
16. *The Holly Tree* (1855).
17. *A Tale of Two Cities* (1859).
18. *Great Expectations* (1860).
19. *Our Mutual Friend* (1864).
20. *The Mystery of Edwin Drood* (1870).

Charles Dickens.

As a footnote, both authors of this book worked on the 1983 film version of *A Christmas Carol*; Maureen assisted the director Clive Donner by coaching the child actors and Kieran played the on-screen role of Peter Cratchit. In fact, he clearly remembers sitting in his Victorian garb reading the Bible to his screen family. It was in a fake Victorian house built in the middle of a huge warehouse on an industrial estate in Telford. Furthermore, as a teacher of history he often makes reference to some of Dickens' works because of their historical importance. *Great Expectations*, of course, is particularly important in promoting a meritocratic social sentiment. After all, if Kit can make it, so can anyone!

J.K. Rowling, b. 1965

This chapter has celebrated the best of British writers from years gone by, but the success of contemporary British writer J.K. Rowling cannot be overlooked. Her Harry Potter series has become the best-selling book series in literary history. The series comprises seven books and an eighth installment in the form of a play. It has also been accompanied by film adaptations and three other associated publications. The fourth installment, *The Goblet of Fire*, became the fastest-selling book in history. Joanne Rowling was born in Yate, in Gloucestershire, and adopted the writing name J.K. Rowling to include her grandmother's name, Kathleen. The idea of Harry Potter and stories of wizardry first came to Rowling in 1990 when she was travelling by train from Manchester to London after a brief spell as a teacher abroad. Following the breakdown of her marriage to a Portuguese journalist, Rowling ended up as a single mum on benefits supporting her little girl in a flat in Edinburgh. This prompted her to start writing the first Harry Potter novel, *Harry Potter and the Philosopher's Stone*, often using a typewriter while sitting in various cafes. By the end of the decade Rowling was a worldwide literary superstar! The Harry Potter books comprise:

1. *Harry Potter and the Philosopher's Stone* (1997).
2. *Harry Potter and the Chamber of Secrets* (1998).
3. *Harry Potter and the Prisoner of Azkaban* (1999).
4. *Harry Potter and the Goblet of Fire* (2000).
5. *Harry Potter and the Order of the Phoenix* (2003).
6. *Harry Potter and the Half-Blood Prince* (2005).
7. *Harry Potter and the Deathly Hallows* (2007).
8. *Harry Potter and the Cursed Child, Parts I and II* (2016; Jack Thorne wrote the play).
9. *Fantastic Beasts and Where to Find Them* (2001).
10. *Quidditch Through The Ages* (2001).
11. *The Tales of Beedle the Bard* (2008).

Other works by Rowling include:

1. *The Casual Vacancy* (2012).
2. *The Cuckoo's Calling* (writing under the pseudonym Robert Galbraith) (2013).
3. *The Silkworm* (as Robert Galbraith) (2014).
4. *Career of Evil* (as Robert Galbraith) (2015).

J.K. Rowling has received many honours and awards, including:

1. Author of the Year and Lifetime Achievement Award and British Book Awards (1999 and 2008).
2. Booksellers Association Author of the Year (1998 and 1999).

3. Order of the British Empire (OBE for service to children's literature) (2001).
4. British Book Awards, Outstanding Achievement (2008).
5. Hans Christian Andersen Literature Award (2010).
6. Numerous honorary degrees and literary prizes.

J.K. Rowling is also a generous philanthropist. In 2000, Rowling established the Volant Charitable Trust to fight poverty and social inequality. The trust's website identifies several areas of funding:

> Charities and projects, whether national or community-based, at home or abroad, that alleviate social deprivation, with a particular emphasis on women's and children's issues.
>
> The Trustees have chosen to fund major disaster appeals as the focus of the Trust's International support.
>
> Research into the causes, treatment and possible cures of Multiple Sclerosis.
>
> J.K. Rowling is supporting major research and treatment into neuro regeneration and Multiple Sclerosis through the University of Edinburgh. The Anne Rowling Regenerative Neurology Clinic opened in 2013 following a substantial donation made by J.K. Rowling in 2010.

Source: https://www.volanttrust.com. Rowling's mother Anne died in 1990 after a ten-year battle with multiple sclerosis.

Chapter 8

Education

Famous British Schools

Britain is known throughout the world as the country of good manners, the country of true ladies and gentlemen, and of course this reputation has to start somewhere, apart from in the home, and that is within the education system. Britain has a wonderful and varied system of educating the young. There is first-class, and free, state education to which every child in the country is entitled. There are variations of course within this system both in execution and achievement but it is there for all. Then there is the private system where parents choose the school that suits their needs, their child's needs and, of course, one that suits the limitations of their pockets too. Into this fee-paying category, or rather at the top of this fee-paying category, falls the British public school system.

Documented in historical archives, renowned throughout the world and revered by some in the home country, the public school is a huge part of British heritage. The cost of a public-school education is prohibitive for most but for some reason is a fascination to most too. Public schools are a bastion of tradition which of course is at the very heart of the British way of life; they are also at the very foundation of wealth and privilege which many hope will by luck or good fortune one day come their way. However, winning the lottery does not necessarily mean that one's children can be educated in these magnificent bastions of education, for as well as extremely lucky one would also have to be clairvoyant and have predicted the good fortune sufficiently early enough to be able to register the child's name at birth! Some of the top British public schools include: Cheltenham Ladies' College, Wycombe Abbey School, Godstowe Preparatory School and Gordonstoun.

Chapter 9

Travel

Rules of the London Underground

First, there is some logic to the routes of the Underground's various lines. It is possible to look at the map and see which lines and station you need to use. London buses, on the other hand, seem to have little logic and are very confusing. If you are a 'local' then you will know which bus to get to reach your particular part of London. The London Underground (also known as the Tube) network is made up of eleven lines, all connected at some point to each other and the train stations above the ground.

Underground Lines on the Tube Map

Underground Line	Colour on the Map
Bakerloo	Brown
Central	Red
Circle	Yellow
District	Green
Hammersmith & City Line	Pink
Jubilee	Grey
Metropolitan	Purple
Northern	Black
Piccadilly	Dark blue
Victoria	Light blue
Waterloo & City Line	Turquoise

However, visitors and new residents shouldn't even bother to try and work it out for a long time! Here are some helpful tips for those not used to travelling on London's Tube network.

1. Get an Oyster card, which saves Tube travellers a lot of money.
2. Do not make eye contact with your fellow travellers – people generally want to be left alone.
3. If you are disabled, elderly or pregnant, do not expect someone to give up your seat for you; this is the exception rather than the rule. Many miserable and stressed out Londoners are either a) too selfish or b) too scared to speak to you (see 2 above).
4. Have your ticket ready to present to the entrance or exit machine as there will be several thousand people behind you all in a deathly hurry; they will have no patience.
5. Make sure you are going in the right direction, even if you have selected the correct line. They can look exactly the same north–south bound and east–west bound.
6. Do not take the signs literally on the platform when they promise you that your train is 3 minutes away. The London Underground minutes are often a lot longer than 60 seconds.
7. At peak times do not see a crowded train coming towards you and say 'we'll get the next one, it might be slightly less full'. No, it will not! Get on whilst you can, whilst it is running, whilst there is no strike, emergency or any other excuse not to run.
8. If London Underground drivers and support staff are on strike, do not go into London. They like to strike on a regular basis over anything from a mouldy sandwich, a stray dog on the platform or because there is a Y in the day of the week. Many are completely oblivious to the chaos they cause and have brought London to a standstill on many occasion. Of course, they always blame their employers for being unreasonable. It clearly had nothing to do with a hard line, militant desire to throw their weight around. The sooner all London Underground trains are made driverless, just like the Docklands Railway, the better!
9. On the moving escalator you must stand on the right so demented people desperate to get to work or home, and clearly far more important than you, can overtake you.

10. Hold on to the handrail in case some jack ass behind you wants to push you; London is home to a lot of weirdos.

11. Wash your hands when you get home as tens of thousands of people have held that handrail and the handrails on the train for that matter.

12. Hold on tight on the train as the carriages lurch forward and throw you around; you could well end up on someone's knee by accident; they won't like it or see the funny side as most people travelling on the Tube have had their sense of humour, compassion, intelligence and spirit surgically removed at the ticket barrier.

13. The defence for the above remark on intelligence comes from the fact that hundreds of people on the platform think they can squeeze onto a full train and not allow passengers off first – they never learn and always ignore the desperate sound of the station announcer calling out in anger 'let the passengers off the train first'.

14. Do not try and use the connecting door between carriages – you will either be fined or killed.

15. There a few London Underground stations that sound ridiculous. Nobody is trying to poke fun at you, these are real stations: Mudchute, Burnt Oak, Cockfosters, Finsbury Park – spelt backwards is Krapy rub snif, Upton Park – Krap Not Pu – this is a good game to play on a long Tube/Underground journey!

Chapter 10

Customs and Traditions

Before exploring the customs and traditions of Great Britain it is necessary first to understand the meaning of, and difference between, the two terms. A custom is the usual and expected mode of behaviour in a particular place, at a particular time; this could be a way that may not be expected or indeed even tolerated in another place or time. A tradition, on the other hand, is a custom, an opinion or a belief that has been handed down from one generation to the next – a sort of custom with staying power. Added to the mix of customs and traditions are particular ways of doing things in Great Britain, ways that are quaint, interesting and ways that are just plain bizarre; put them all together and you have a charmingly idiosyncratic race of people.

Etiquette

> 'Manners Maketh Man'
> William of Wykeham (1324–1404),
> the motto of Winchester College
> and New College, Oxford

The British people are known the world over for their good manners and reserved nature, so the saying 'Manners maketh man' sits really well in British culture and way of life. 'Thank you' are two of the first words a young child is taught to say and even when a toddler is given an ice cream – for which his mother has paid – he is still encouraged with 'Say thank you to the nice man', the underlying threat being that if he doesn't the ice cream will mysteriously disappear! Maureen's children's Christmas stockings always included a box of thank-you notelets and if we didn't start writing them on Boxing Day then we knew that our presents would start to disappear just as mysteriously and quickly as Father Christmas had brought them! A little harsh, but we turned out to be very polite children, and saying thank you either verbally or by letter has become second nature. Is this because we are British? We like to use the expression 'please' and 'thank you' quite a lot.

Greetings

Of course it doesn't all revolve around the above mentioned words either. Let's start with that first meeting. In Britain the kiss, unlike many other countries, is reserved primarily for close family members, or those you genuinely love! It is not considered the correct way in which to great an acquaintance or – heaven forbid – a stranger. As with many things, there are regional variations and you are more likely to be kissed by 'someone you don't love' in the South of the British Isles than in the North, as you are more likely to be greeted with a kiss by someone in the acting profession than by a builder! So if you are greeted by an actor in the South be prepared for a kiss – ONE kiss though, for there are still limitations even to this. So if the kiss is a no-go area how do the British greet each other? With a nice firm handshake, of course, right hand to right hand; even children are encouraged to shake the hand of a stranger when first introduced.

So now you know not to kiss but to shake hands, what do you actually say to the other person? Well, if you don't know them, or have possibly never met them before, then the correct salutation is: 'How do you do'. Which, actually, is not a question but a greeting and so the other person replies with, 'How do you do' as well. You have to feel sorry for the visitors to British shores, don't you, for so much of what we do makes little sense at all!

Eating

Table manners in Britain are very important, even in the privacy of one's own home, though they are more relaxed now than a few decades ago. Even as recently as the 1960s and 1970s children in many homes were expected to adhere to a strict set of rules – and of course some families have hung on to a few, and in some cases, even all of them to this day. Such rules include:

- Do not put your elbows on the table.
- Do not start eating your meal until everyone else has been served theirs.
- Do not leave the table until everyone has finished eating and, in the case of children, ask permission to leave with the words: 'Please may I leave the table?'

In Britain a knife and fork is used to eat a meal and it is considered rude to use one without the other. When eating bread, it is also considered impolite to eat the bread whole or indeed to cut it with a knife; a small piece must always be broken off and then eaten either dry or buttered. Soup is consumed by tipping the bowl away from you and by eating the soup from the side of the spoon – unlike other countries where diners eat from the end of the spoon. When you have finished eating – not taking a break – you indicate this to others at your table or to a waiter when in a restaurant. There are of course many more rules for the very picky, or for those who are sticklers for correctness, but the ones mentioned here are the very foundations upon which good British table manners are built.

Social Behaviour

When out and about the British continue to be reserved and reasonably quiet, in comparison with many of their European neighbours, that is. It is still considered polite for a gentleman to remove his hat when entering a building and many of the older generation will still tip their hat when greeting – and sometimes just simply passing – a lady; this is a charming custom and is a display of the genteel manners for which we are renowned throughout the world. A gentleman travelling by public transport would still be expected to offer his seat to any lady standing and when out and about to open doors for ladies and the elderly; children and young people similarly would be expected to do the same. Sadly, this tradition is in rapid decline.

Quotations

When you feel like giving up and charging through life in some sort of random and discourteous way then read through a few of the quotations below and you may find that journeying on the straight and narrow is in fact more fun than you first thought.

> Good manners will open doors that the best education cannot.
>
> Clarence Thomas

> We don't bother much about dress and manners in England, because as a nation we don't dress well and we've no manners.
>
> George Bernard Shaw

> Politeness and consideration for others is like investing pennies and getting dollars back.
>
> Thomas Sowell

Queues

They do say that when the British are abroad and they see two people standing next to each other they either get very excited or very nostalgic, the reason for this being that they believe they are seeing the beginning of a queue! This has to be what the British do best and it has become the British way of life. The actual word 'queue' comes from French, and in turn from the Latin word *cauda*, which means 'tail'. The British just love to stand in an orderly queue – they queue for buses, the cinema, ice creams, in fact anything at all where two or more people are waiting for the same thing is deemed a queue. To a British citizen, whether at home or abroad, it is downright rude not to stand in an orderly queue and a mortal sin to 'push in', which is the British word for queue jumping.

Why are there always queues in Britain? First, there are constant roadworks; many are left over night, on long weekends and holidays without any work actually taking place. Secondly, it seems as though few people have a sense of urgency in the bank or Post Office, taking as long as they want and usually retired people going in during the lunch break. Thirdly, many people seem so oblivious that it is their turn next that they just stand there with the queue shouting at them.

There does seem to be a different way of queueing depending on what country you are in. If you go to Turkey, for example, God help you if you leave more than a centimetre between you and the person in front of you. You get those behind you shouting at you to move forward or even trying to fill the gap. In France, it seems to be a national sport to just come along and push your way in front of whoever is already there.

Cricket

Each of the countries in Britain has its own customs and traditions, respected by the sister countries but undeniably their own. In England one of the traditional games played is cricket. Mention the word to an Englishman and even for the most un-sporty of them it will conjure up images of a slow and genteel summer's afternoon on the village green, the sound of a ball on willow and the thought of afternoon tea prepared and served on the terrace by the players' wives; all so English and all so perfectly tranquil. Now ask the same people to explain to you the rules of the game and you will be met by a sea of blank faces. It seems that very few people actually understand the rules of this very English game. Read the explanation (taken from melcarson.com) below and then see whether you can understand them!

- You have two sides, one out in the field and one in.
- Each man that's in the side that's in goes out, and when he's out he comes in and the next man goes in until he's out.
- When they are all out, the side that's out comes in and the side that's been in goes out and tries to get those coming in out.
- Sometimes you get men still in and not out.
- When a man goes out to go in, the men who are out try to get him out, and when he is out he goes in and the next man in goes out and goes in.
- There are two men called umpires who stay out all the time and they decide when the men who are in are out.
- When both sides have been in and all the men have been out, and both sides have been out twice after all the men have been in, including those who are not out, that is the end of the game! Simple?

Cheese Rolling at Coopers Hill

Some people think that the tradition of cheese rolling at Coopers Hill in Gloucestershire stretches back hundreds, even thousands, of years and is thought to have its roots in a heathen festival to celebrate the return of spring, whilst others believe it to be a pagan healing ritual. But who knows the truth and actual origins behind this bizarre event? No one it would appear, so let's just accept the speculation and conjecture as a part of the event and turn to the actual tradition of the cheese rolling, starting with an explanation of the event itself.

- Competitors race down a steep hill, the object being to catch an 8lb Double Gloucester cheese; the cheese has been released before the competitors set off after it and can reach speeds of over 100km an hour!
- The race involves those taking part tumbling, somersaulting and scrambling their way down the hill before the cheese is finally 'grabbed' by the winner.
- The hill is actually a 1:2 gradient in places, even 1:1, and injuries are frequently sustained during the event, such as sprains and broken bones.
- This annual event is usually held on the May Spring Bank Holiday weekend.

The event has been growing in popularity and media coverage over the past ten or so years and now attracts many more participants and spectators each year and from all around the world. About 3 miles away from the event, in the town of Shurdington, there is a pub named The Cheese Rollers, where tactics and strategy planning can be discussed before each race.

Maypole Dancing

This is essentially a very picturesque event, taking place on village greens around England – picturesque that is if the sun shines, the maypole is securely fixed in the ground and the dancers don't get into a tangled mess with the ribbons that they thread around the pole as a part of the dancing! Traditionally, it all starts when the winter ends; trees are cut down and stuck into the ground for the villagers – well actually it is usually the children of the villagers – to dance around heralding the start of summer and the planting of the crops. Just like cricket, there is a feel and an atmosphere that is inexplicably attached to Maypole dancing and to even just watch it makes the spectator feel a part of the British way of life.

Some traditions in the British calendar are unique to the nation but others are noted in other countries too: Bonfire Night, morris dancing, bank holidays, Burns' Night, Edinburgh Festival, goose fair, Halloween, Maundy Thursday, April Fool's Day, village greens, May Day, Mothering Sunday, first footing, Remembrance Sunday, pancake day, St George's Day, St Patrick's Day, St Swithin's Day, Trooping of the Colour, Changing of the Guard and Valentine's Day.

Chapter 11

Phoneboxes and Postboxes

The Red Telephone Box

The red public telephone box, designed by Sir Giles Gilbert Scott, has been a familiar sight on the streets of the UK since 1926. However, the first public payphones appeared in 1920. At its peak of popularity in the 1980s, there were more than 73,000 phoneboxes. Over the years the red phonebox became an iconic British piece of architecture, well known and easily identifiable as British. However, with the advent of mobile phones many became little used or even neglected and thousands have since been sold off to private buyers. When British Telecom said they were no longer useful and continued

(*Photo: Kieran Hughes*)

removing them, journalist Cristina Odone protested that 'nationhood is about more than purpose; it is about tradition, ritual, and symbol' (*Telegraph*, 11 March 2013). This is exactly why the symbol of the red phonebox has been included in this book, because of it being synonymous with Britishness.

The Red Postbox

This has also become one of Britain's iconic designs and is recognised across the world. However, there were many variations before this system was established. The Penny Post opened up the postal system to everyone from

1840. People were no longer expected to take their letters to a receiving house (rather like an early post office). Nor were they expected to wait for the bellman, who came around once a day ringing his bell and collecting letters to post. The Post Office decided to pinch the Continental idea of roadside boxes for people to drop off their letters.

A trial was started in the Channel Islands in 1853 and eventually expanded to mainland Britain. Local surveyors were given responsibility for designing the boxes and a number of these appeared over the years. They were individual and inconsistent. Not only was the design an ongoing experiment, but the colour

(*Photo: Kieran Hughes*)

became a rather contentious issue. They were red to start with and then green by 1859. The idea of green pillar boxes came about so that they were visually unobtrusive in the landscape. However, this consideration backfired because so many people complained that they were hard to find. The Post Office then started to change them to chocolate brown but this proved too expensive so someone suggested that bright red remain the standardised colour. This was introduced in 1874 and the nationwide re-painting process took ten years to complete. There have also been countless designs of postboxes over the years. However, the reign of Queen Elizabeth II has seen the biggest variety of designs since those early Victorian experiments. After Britain's success in the 2012 London Olympic Games, a number of red postal boxes were repainted gold.

Chapter 12

Britain's Beaches

Being an island means that Britain is spoilt for choice when it comes to waterside retreats and seaside fun. It would be impossible to include all the great places in Britain here, but there follows a good selection as well as mention of the many seaside traditions Britain is famous for.

Rhossili Bay, Wales

With miles and miles of golden sands, he *Independent* described Rhossili as 'the supermodel of British beaches'. It remains a favourite for sunbathers, surfers and walkers, and was also once voted Britain's best beach by TripAdvisor. This breathtaking environment is the most westerly bay on the Gower peninsula and features a huge expanse of beach exposed during low tide, encouraging long seaside walks.

Scarborough, Yorkshire

Once regarded as the Costa del Sol of the North East, this was 'the' place to be in the summer time with your family from the 1950s–70s. Its long sandy beaches and miles of arcades, cafes and gift shops encapsulate the perfect, traditional seaside town.

Armadale Bay Beach

Pure sand enclosed by two rocky headlands, stunning views and unimaginable peace are just some of the ways to describe one of the most beautiful beaches in Scotland. The weather in Scotland may not always encourage people to strip down to swimwear but the two headlands do cut off some of the winds, making it an enjoyable place to visit. It is popular with walkers and surfers yet remains unspoilt. Openroadscotland.com whilst reminding us of the 6,000 miles of beaches in Scotland (excluding islands) is keen to include Armadale as one of its most recommended beaches. Undiscoveredscotland. co.uk describes Armadale's views as 'outstanding'.

The Great British Seaside Getaway

Sandcastles, ice cream, kiss-me-quick hats and of course windbreakers for the poor weather are all synonymous with the great British seaside. Generations of children have ventured to the sandy beaches of Britain for an exciting day's adventure or even a mini-holiday. It was once the staple of family sunshine breaks before the advent of cheap foreign trips. There was a time when it was assumed one would holiday at home, along Britain's coastline. It was not until the 1950s that holidaying abroad really took off. Even as late as the 1930s and 1940s more than 15 million people visited the seaside each year. Even by the 1970s record numbers of Brits were holidaying on the British coastline. The early days of coastline indulgence in places like Blackpool, Whitby and Scarborough spread throughout the British Isles during Victorian and Edwardian times. The advent of the passenger train network made it possible for people to get to the coast and later the motor car encouraged a new wave of visitors. Uninhibited fun and frolics on the sand was a gradual but significant social and cultural shift and one that influenced similar patterns abroad.

Another reason that the seaside is a desired 'resting' destination is a deep-seated psychological belief in associating water with good health. The Romans used spas for washing, resting and socialising, perhaps the most famous of these being the town of Bath. However, this notion vanished with our Roman invaders a few hundred years later. It was not until the European Renaissance that the idea of spas returned to cultural normality. Rich Englishmen visited the health spas on the Continent until Georgian times. After that, the idea came back to Britain. Once again, good health, relaxation and happiness were associated with water. Therefore, the Victorian desire to visit the sea was in part underpinned by this emotional attachment to water. In other words, people visited the seaside to be next to the water, and you don't get more water than in the ocean! It has never been an off-beat idea to link water to healing.

Beach Huts

Beach huts at Bournemouth. (*Photos: Hugh Mothersole*)

Only in Britain would people spend more money on a beach hut than on a proper house. A feeling of nostalgia and the love of the sea on this lovely island has replenished the nation's interest in what was once a modesty saving Edwardian necessity. At the turn of the century over dressed men and women bathed on separate beaches and getting changed was carried out in the privacy of a bathing machine (a private, portable changing room). The machine was pushed out to sea so the bather could get into the water without being seen by anyone. By the second decade of the twentieth century, social expectations had started to change. Beaches full of both sexes in bathing costumes became an acceptable sight. However, people still needed somewhere to change, as getting changed under a towel, coat or blanket on the beach was not deemed appropriate social behaviour. Therefore, councils started to provide beach huts for this purpose. Today, the huts are more about convenience, pride, occasional snobbery and, in some cases, investment. They are often painted in pretty colours, have a kettle and a fridge and provide a safe place to change or keep valuables.

Piers

Britain is famous for its seaside piers and the character and charm they add to resorts. At the start of the twentieth century there were almost a hundred structures gracing the coastline. A hundred years later, half have gone and several more are fighting for their survival. The evolution of the seaside pier was a result of the ingenuity and achievement of the best Victorian engineers. In recent years many piers have faced the threat of closure and demolition. Britain's National Piers Society was founded in 1979 and has since become the leading authority on piers, campaigning extensively for their preservation for generations to come.

Candyfloss

This sugar-rich, teeth-decaying seaside snack was invented by an American dentist – you couldn't make it up! In South Africa it is actually called 'tooth floss' and the American name is 'cotton candy'. According to the *New York Times*, it 'is almost 99.999 percent sugar, with a little flavoring and food coloring'. It can be seen hanging up in bags at the seaside or children can watch it being made in a circular machine and then stuck on a stick. It might be an American invention, but as that is actually in dispute, it can be classed as a British tradition.

Donkey Rides at the Seaside

Children riding on a donkey up and down the beach is a familiar sight, although a declining one. This too was a Victorian idea and came about because donkeys were working draught animals in the cockle industries operating around the coast. Most donkeys have their names displayed so children can return to have another ride on their 'favourite'. Other childhood seaside traditions include: kiss-me-quick hats, arcades, buckets and spades and the Punch and Judy show. All of these elements have together been the basis of British seaside culture, although now they are being gradually replaced by fast-food joints, coffee shops and other more 'sophisticated' additions, thus changing this once interesting part of Britain's heritage.

Punch and Judy

This seems to be another fading seaside tradition. Although technically Italian in its roots, it has been adopted as a British cultural addition to the seaside. Critics have often complained about the 'violence' as Mr Punch goes about beating his adversaries.

Saucy Seaside Postcards

Many deltiologists are keen to collect Britain's saucy seaside postcards, with a cheeky message and funny cartoon. They are often risqué and full of innuendo, thus stretching Britain's moral standards and in turn attracting the critics. Bawdy humour on a postcard was started by Donald McGill in 1912. Postcards had been around in Britain from 1894 but it took a few years to realise that the best design was a message and the address (and stamp) on one side and a picture on the other side. McGill's saucy postcard career was a huge success, with 200 million cards with 12,000 of his funny designs sold. The new saucy seaside postcards became part of Britain's holiday culture, selling 16 million a year at their peak. A company called Bamforth also produced a series of saucy seaside postcards. James Bamforth was the son of a Yorkshire painter and decorator who used his photography and postcard-making skills to comment on themes such as sex, drinking and marriage, but always with innuendo. In the 1950s, a concerned Conservative government attempted a crackdown on this deltiological immorality. Many of these new politically incorrect cards were deemed too suggestive for their day. McGill even faced obscenity charges over his postcards in 1954 and was fined £50 by local magistrates. Government censorship during a clean-up period of seaside towns labelled many of McGill's cards as 'obscene' and were stamped with 'disproved for sale' by the Postcard Censoring Committee.

Favourite Resorts

The Victorian seaside resorts served a purpose, by supplying the demands of an expanding class. First came the shop workers and office clerks with extra income, followed by a working-class army of hard-working factory staff, often in need of a break from long and physically demanding work. A growing population always wants more. The seaside break was the nation's way of taking a well-earned rest. A survey in *Which?* magazine listed its own top seaside resorts:

1. Blackpool.
2. Brighton.
3. Whitby.

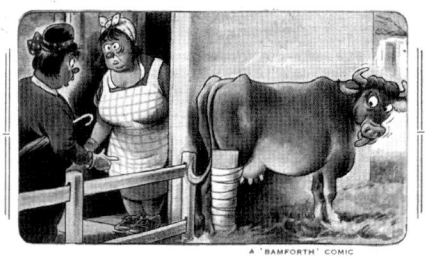

(*Images supplied by David Benson*)

  4. Bournemouth.
  5. Scarborough.
  6. Newquay.
  7. Torquay.
  8. St Ives.
  9. Skegness.
10. Great Yarmouth.

A tripadvisor.co.uk survey ranked British beaches in the following order:

  1. Woolacombe Beach.
  2. Weymouth Beach.
  3. St Brelade's Bay Beach.
  4. Rhossili Bay.
  5. Porthmeor Beach, St Ives.
  6. Fistral Beach, Newquay .
  7. Porthminster Beach, St Ives.
  8. Perranporth Beach.
  9. Hengistbury Head, Bournemouth.
10. Luskentyre, Outer Hebrides.

Chapter 13

The Best of British Designs and Inventions

In 1933, Yorkshire road contractor Percy Shaw came up with the idea of cats' eyes in the middle of the road to aid vision at night. He claimed that the invention was the result of a foggy night's drive after an evening out when he noticed the reflection of his headlights in the eyes of a real cat.

In 1989, Sir Tim Berners-Lee invented the world wide web (not quite the same as the Internet). The Internet already existed as a network of joined up computers. Berners-Lee developed a server in 1990 and by 1991 the web went live. He did not charge for his invention but has since been recognised with a knighthood. This one invention has changed the lives of most people in the world. He came up with the term 'world wide web'.

In 1876, Aexander Graham Bell patented his design for the telephone after discovering that a thin vibrating metal sheet in an electromagnetic field makes an electrical waveform.

The cash dispenser has been used by most people in the world but started off as a brain wave of John Shepherd-Barron in 1967. Barclays was the first bank to sign up to the new invention, installing the first machine outside its Enfield branch the same year. The maximum withdrawal was limited to £10. The idea of a four-digit pin number was used from the very start.

The London Underground map is one of the most easily recognised symbols in the world and has been seen by billions of people over the decades. Harry Beck, an electrical circuit designer for the London Passenger Transport Board, designed the map in the 1930s after disregarding the relative distance between the stations. Bosses on the Tube originally feared that the image was far too radical and would be rejected.

The Royal Marsden Cancer Hospital

The word famous British cancer hospital the Royal Marsden is the result of the idea of one man. British surgeon William Marsden (1796–1867) was born in Sheffield in 1796 and as a young man travelled to London to work in the fields of medicine and pharmacy. Whilst working at St Bartholomew's hospital, Marsden served an apprenticeship to a surgeon in Holborn and also studied anatomy.

One simple event in 1827 changed the course of medical history. Marsden found a young girl aged 18 on the steps of St Andrew's Church. Despite her serious condition, including malnourishment and disease, he was unable to get her hospital treatment without a letter of recommendation. Marsden was appalled by the system and decided to establish his own medical practice and in 1828 opened a small dispensary in Greville Street, a place where the poor could receive simple medical assistance without any letter of recommendation. Marsden felt patients were not getting a good deal with the current system, and he demanded an end to fees and letters of recommendation. Marsden was faced with much opposition because he treated the poor, those with cholera and even prostitutes. He treated those that the main hospitals refused to help. Marsden's early work was carried out while Edwin Chadwick was gathering evidence on public health. There was debate linking squalor to health and miasma was still a popular theory.

Marsden's wealthy friends purchased a site in Gray's Inn Road in 1843 and a new bigger hospital was built. In 1843 the Royal Free Hospital (London General Institution was its original name) opened its doors. Marsden became the hospital's senior surgeon. He wanted to do things differently in a rapidly emerging early nineteenth-century medical market, changing the way things were done forever. He went against culture and tradition. His early endeavours are carefully preserved in the hospital's *Board of Governors' Minutes* and the *Committee of Management Minutes*, of 1828.

The primary sources show how the Royal Free called other London hospitals 'incompetent' and questioned delays at getting seen, declaring that sick people were being turned away. The hospital's board stated that 'instant relief and constant attention are of the utmost importance'. It criticises the on-going policies of restriction and regulations regarding admissions. Many hospitals only saw their out-patients once a week. Marsden said that this was inadequate and that his organisation aimed to see patients twice a day. Marsden's team made another political statement in relation to supporting a free hospital, saying 'if benevolence and religion did not recommend an institution, let us do it for selfish reasons, to keep alive industrious, valuable members of society'.

In 1832 the Royal Free reiterated its policy on referrals by stating 'no ticket or recommendation from a subscriber is necessary to be provided … poverty and disease alone are the wretched qualifications'. Marsden was a determined character, not afraid of pushing the acceptable boundaries of the day if he thought things could be improved. He defied the opposition and made people understand that everyone was entitled to be treated, whatever their condition, financial status or social connections. The impact of this one man has been enormous and has changed the history of medicine. His ideas and values were like that of the NHS, 120 years ahead of its inauguration.

Marsden and his team's treatment of cholera and venereal disease demonstrate how he worked to help those who were most in need, as stated in the primary sources, and his attack on those who did not help. During the 1832 cholera epidemic most hospitals were closing their doors to victims, but the Royal Free was welcoming them. There was a public debate about keeping sufferers separate, but the Royal Free was putting them together, with cholera wards in existence by 1846. There was friction between Marsden and other hospitals about whether cholera patients should be admitted and kept together. It was a field of contested ideas over contagion. There were great epidemiological and pathological debates, and advances, throughout the first half of the nineteenth century. The 1832 epidemic was before Chadwick's report and the final plans for sanitary reform. It was before an aetiological approach to cholera, seventeen years before Jon Snow's water theory in Soho (accepted after 1866) and almost fifty years before Robert Koch's identification of the etiological microbe that caused cholera. The uncertainty is evident in the fact that more than sixty years after Marsden opened his doors to cholera patients, the Royal College of Physicians was still not advising people to boil their water. The uncertainty in the medical world about whether this was right was understandable. The 1832 epidemic was way before the emergence of the germ theory and at the time Marsden was admitting cholera patients, the miasma theory was often favoured.

Marsden announced more help would be given to VD sufferers. He denied that helping them would encourage them and promote bad behaviour. Marsden declared that 'wretched females who frequent the streets have always been welcome ... the more wretched they are, and the more diseased, the greater is their claim on this charity'. It was an attack on the other hospitals that morally judged these women. The Royal Free said, 'these poor girls enticed from their country homes, seduced, diseased, abandoned ... have no shelter or refuge left to them save within the walls of institutions similar to the Royal Free'.

Marsden's early days are framed by social changes and attitudes, and an emerging medical market with limited control until the 1858 Medical Act. There was little understanding of the danger of germs and bacteria. By criticising hospitals for not taking in cholera or VD patients during a period of scientific, epidemiological and pathological changes, Marsden was showing his disapproval of the medical establishment.

Marsden's wife Betsy-Ann died of cancer in 1846, and he now turned his attention to this disease. In 1851, he opened a small house in Cannon Row, Westminster, for the reception of cancer patients. At first Cannon Row consisted solely of a dispensary prescribing palliative drugs. However, this was just the start and Marsden was determined to study cancerous tumours, find the causes and discover new treatments for patients. The hospital soon outgrew the Cannon Row premises and generous benefactors enabled a specially built hospital to open in Brompton. In 1910 it became known as the Cancer Hospital (Free). Later, King Edward VIII added the word 'Royal' and in 1954 the hospital was renamed the Royal Marsden Hospital in recognition of the work of William Marsden. In 1948, it was taken over by the newly formed NHS. A second hospital in Sutton, Surrey, was opened in 1962.

The Royal Marsden Hospital has become the world's leading cancer hospital, offering pioneering treatment, surgery, medication, trials and after-care. People travel from all over the country, and even further afield to be treated at the Royal Marsden. It is certainly something Britain should be proud of. Its website states, 'The world's first hospital dedicated to cancer diagnosis, treatment, research and education.' It also, proudly declares, 'At the Royal Marsden, we deal with cancer every day so we understand how valuable life is. and when people entrust their lives to us, they have the right to demand the very best. Leading cancer research and treatment since 1851.' It treats 50,000 patients a year, free of charge. It does, however, ask for people to take part in fund-raising events. It has access to more cancer drugs, treatment and expertise than any other hospital. It extends lives and saves lives, day in, day out. It certainly qualifies for the title 'Best of British'. History can change in a split second. If William Marsden's wife had not died of cancer, then the world's leading cancer hospital and research centre in London and Surrey would probably not be in existence today. The death of Betsy-Ann from cancer has changed cancer treatment for thousands of patients.

On a sad note, in relation to the worst of British selfishness, in 2008 some neighbours of the Sutton cancer hospital opposed £15 million plans to turn part of the Royal Marsden Hospital there into a leading teenage cancer treatment centre in the UK. Local residents complained about the noise these young cancer patients might make on a dedicated roof-top terrace. The complainants raised concerns about reception for their television aerials, extra traffic and the possibility of it all having a negative impact on the value of their properties.

The historiography of William Marsden is limited, but includes: Lynne A. Amidon, *An Illustrated History of the Royal Free Hospital* (1996); Frieda Sandwith, *Surgeon Compassionate* (1960), a biography by Marsden's great-granddaughter; Eve Wiltshaw, *A History of The Royal Marsden* (1998), about his later life post-1851.

Chapter 14

The Arts

The Artists William Turner and John Constable

John Constable (11 June 1776–31 March 1837) is most famous for his paintings *Dedham Vale* (1802) and *The Hay Wain* (1821). Joseph Mallord William Turner (23 April 1775–19 December 1851) is most famous for his paintings *The Slave Ship* (1840) and *The Fighting Temeraire* (1839).

These British landscape artists were pioneers of a revolutionary style of landscape painting, creating a romantic response to nature and capturing its spirit rather than concentrating on accuracy. Constable told a friend, 'painting is but another word for feeling'. Turner's complex ideas were inspired by his extensive travels, whereas Constable, who never left England, became known for his depiction of rural scenes. Where they differed in technique, family background, temperament (Constable was known for his rebellious attitude) and even looks, they shared a love of nature. The competition between these two painters could be described as one of the greatest ever artistic rivalries. It was both personal and professional. Even so, both men are worthy of places in the 'Best of British' hall of fame. The question is, which artist do you prefer?

A selection of Constable's paintings:

Boat-building near Flatford Mill (1815).
Portrait of Maria Bicknell, Mrs John Constable (1816).
Wivenhoe Park, Essex (1816).
The White Horse Hampstead Heath (1819).
Stratford Mill (1820).
View on the Stour, near Dedham (1822).
Salisbury Cathedral from the Bishop's Grounds (1825).
The Lock (1824).

Seascape Study with Rain Clouds (1824–5).
Brighton Beach (*c.* 1824–6).
The Leaping Horse (1825).
The Cornfield (1826).
Dedham Vale (1802).
Hadleigh Castle (1829).
Salisbury Cathedral from the Meadows (1831).

A selection of Turner's paintings:

The Battle of Trafalgar, as Seen from the Mizen Starboard Shrouds of the Victory (1806).
The Trout Stream (1809).
Snow Storm: Hannibal and His Army Crossing the Alps (1812).
Crossing the Brook (1815).
Eruption of Vesuvius (1817).
Raby Castle, the Seat of the Earl of Darlington (1817).
The Battle of Trafalgar (1822).
Cologne: The Arrival of a Packet-Boat (1826).
Ulysses Deriding Polyphemus (1829).
The Fountain of Indolence (1834).
The Burning of the Houses of Lords and Commons (1835).
The Grand Canal, Venice (1835).
The Piazzetta, Venice (1835).
Juliet and Her Nurse (1836).
Mercury and Argus (1836).
The Fighting Temeraire (1839).
Neapolitan Fisher Girls Surprised Bathing by Moonlight (1840).
The Blue Rigi, Sunrise (1842).
Snow Storm: Steam-Boat off a Harbour's Mouth (1842).
The Evening of the Deluge (1843).

Before you think about buying one of these paintings, both artists' work can set you back an enormous amount of money – that's if pieces even get to auction. To give you an idea about price, in 2006, Turner's *Giudecca, La Donna della Salute and San Giorgio* sold at auction in New York for $35.8 million. In 2012, John Constable's *The Lock* became one of the most expensive British paintings in history, fetching £22.4m at auction in London.

Elsewhere in the world of the arts, entertainment and sport, Britain can be proud of the greats such as: Sir Paul McCartney, John Lennon, Sir Andrew Lloyd-Webber, Sir Tim Rice, Sir Cameron Mackintosh, Sir Elton John, George Michael, Adele, Simon Cowell, The Spice Girls, Queen, The Rolling Stones, David Bowie, Shirley Bassey, David Beckham, the Two Ronnies, Morecombe and Wise, *Only Fools and Horses* creator John Sullivan, Ray Cooney, Daley Thompson, Lord Sebastian Coe, Steve Ovett, Sir Steve Redgrave, Bobby Moore, Sir Andy Murray, Fred Perry, Sir Jackie Stewart, Sir Nick Faldo, Lennox Lewis and Sir Ian Botham.

Chapter 15

Worship

The Right to Freedom of Worship

Everybody in Britain has the right to choose their own religion, or be an atheist. A person's right to worship without ridicule or harassment is protected and enshrined in law. In 2014, the government took it one step further, to encourage long-term religious tolerance and as a way to reduce and prevent dangerous extremism. The government called this 'strengthening the barriers to extremism'. The document *Guidance on Promoting British Values in Schools* was published by the Conservative and Liberal Democrat coalition government. It highlights the expectation in British society of 'mutual respect and tolerance of those with different faiths and beliefs'. These values were originally set out by the government in 2011 in a document called *Prevent*.

The then Parliamentary Under Secretary of State for Schools Lord Nash stated that he wanted every school 'to promote the basic British values of democracy, the rule of law, individual liberty, and mutual respect and tolerance for those of different faiths and beliefs'. No longer was it acceptable simply to respect other people's religion, schools now had to be proactive and include this social message by embedding it into teaching and learning strategies.

It remains one of the best parts of British culture that a multitude of religions, faiths and beliefs can be embraced. In some parts of the world people can be arrested and punished for their religious beliefs, or lack of them. In Britain, tolerance is the civilised key word to underpin a rounded society of freedom. In practice, Britain has 51,000 churches, 1,500 mosques and 400 synagogues as well as lots of other places of worship. Also, Britain has faith schools where parents can select an education with a certain religious value. In fact, one of the few areas where religious tolerance has not been a way of British life is within royal circles. It is still the case that no Roman Catholic can take the throne.

Until changes in the law in 2013 any member of the royal family who even married a Roman Catholic was barred from the succession. This antiquated system went against all the British values expected by the government and flew in the face of modern acceptability of respect and tolerance. This was simply 'not' the best of British. However, supporters of the antiquated law insisted that it was not through intolerance or bigotry that they backed Roman Catholic exclusion but that it was

Salisbury Cathedral. (*Photo: Kieran Hughes*)

based on political necessity. In other words, this was the same argument that existed in the days of Henry VIII about unacceptable papal jurisdiction over Britain. The practical argument is that a Roman Catholic monarch could not be head of the Church of England.

Britain has some of the best religious buildings in the world. The sheer splendour and eloquence of some of these structures are often staggering. Places such as Durham Cathedral, York Minister, Salisbury Cathedral and Westminster Abbey are breathtaking. Some mosques in places such as Bradford, Birmingham and London can hold over 5,000 worshippers.

Chapter 16

Worst of Britain

The M25 Motorway

The M25 is a 117-mile British motorway that practically encircles Greater London. It was first discussed in 1905 and then in more detail in the 1960s as part of a plan to construct four ring roads around London. A few parts were built in the early 1970s and it was finally completed in 1986. It remains one of the busiest motorways in Europe, passing major junctions such as Heathrow Airport. Regular users might see it as the best of British in that it is a cleverly designed route but it has to make the worst of British because of the extreme queues and constant roadworks.

Local Councils

The unaccountable local authorities that subcontract services, change goal posts, reduce services and treat residents like 'stupid' cash cows just have to make the worst of British list. Some are obstructive, incompetent and unhelpful. Think about potholes, fortnightly rubbish collections, huge council tax bills and the expensive power trip otherwise known as 'planning permission'. We would be better of going back to the Middle Ages, reporting to a lord of the manor!

Parking Wardens

Some of these immoral creatures hide and jump out on you. Nobody knows how they miraculously appear from nowhere. Some are strangely absent when certain people park illegally but are very quick to pounce on anyone who makes a genuine mistake. Some of these vile individuals 'hang out' at postboxes and cashpoints, the services people need the most.

The Weather

Originally the plan was to include 'complaining' in this worst of British section but actually a lot of the complaining and moaning is about the weather. This is fairly justified sometimes. The weather in the UK is awful. As an island surrounded by the sea, England has a varied climate. The inhabitants endure a mixture of rain, sunshine, wind and anything else it throws at them unpredictably and completely changeable from one hour to the next. Summers rarely last the entire summer season and nobody ever knows whether it will be a mild or frosty winter. There is certainly a lot to moan about!

Clamping

If you park your car illegally in Central London, it can be clamped by the local authority, who then tow it away and charge you an extortionate amount of money to get your car back. If you delay getting it back then they will charge you storage and or disposal fees. This is yet another anti-motorist scam against Britain's drivers, fully backed by the government. One good thing that the government changed was to outlaw clamping on private land in England and Wales in 2012. (It has been law in Scotland since 1992.) The Protection of Freedoms Act stopped criminal-like gangs charging hundreds of pounds for people accidentally parking on private land for a few minutes.

(*Image: Dave Brace*)

Did you Know?

- Britain's first hippopotamus in modern times arrived at London Zoo in Regent's Park on 25 May 1850.
- The House of the Plantagenets derives its name from King Henry III who liked to wear a sprig of *planta genista*.
- More than 50,000 guests a year attend banquets, dinners, lunches, receptions and garden parties at Buckingham Palace.
- The Scottish city of Edinburgh is nicknamed 'Auld Reekie', which means 'Old Smokey'.
- Britain was once a republic and so had no king or queen. It happened in 1649, after King Charles I was executed; but it was only an eleven-year wonder for the monarchy was restored to its rightful place at the heart of the British people in 1660.
- There were many very young monarchs in times gone by, for example, Henry III was crowned king when he was just 9 years old and King Henry VI was only 8 months old when he became King of England (and France). Edward VI was 9 years old and in Scotland, Mary, Queen was Scots was just a few days old when she became monarch.
- England's Stonehenge is at least 1,500 years older than Rome's Colosseum.
- The Forth (Railway) Bridge in Scotland is actually a metre longer in the summer months than the winter months; this is due to thermal expansion.
- The phrase 'rule of thumb' is derived from an old English law which stated that a man couldn't beat his wife with anything wider than his thumb.
- In Shakespeare's time, mattresses were secured on bed frames by ropes. When the ropes were pulled the mattress tightened, so making the bed firmer to sleep on. And that's where the phrase 'goodnight, sleep tight' originated.
- Great Britain is the only country in the world that doesn't have the country's name on its postage stamps.
- The military salute comes from medieval knights raising their visors to see each other.
- Queen Anne had eighteen children, all of whom died before she did.
- Big Ben does not refer to the clock, but actually the bell within.

- French was the official language of Great Britain for about 300 years.
- The first British telephone directory published contained just 248 names and no numbers.
- 'The Star Spangled Banner' (the American national anthem) was created by a British man.
- The Queen owns all the sturgeons, whales and dolphins in the waters within 3 miles of the UK.
- J.K. Rowling is the first person to make a billion dollars from writing books.
- James Bond's code '007' was inspired by the author Ian Fleming's bus route from Canterbury to London.
- The London Eye is the 'largest cantilevered observation wheel in the world'.
- Nowhere in the British Isles is more than 75 miles from the sea – although arguments over this have raged for years. No one, however, seems prepared to get out the measuring tape and find the definitive answer. So perhaps it should be: they say that 'apparently' nowhere in the British Isles is more than 75 miles from the sea!
- When Charles II's illegitimate son, the Duke of Monmouth, was executed at the Tower of London, it took five blows of the axe to sever his head from his body
- Margaret Beaufort was only 13 when she gave birth to the future Henry VII. By that time, she had already been married twice.
- Until late Victorian times the age of sexual consent in Britain was 13. It was increased to 16 to try and reduce the problem of children working as prostitutes.

Bibliography

Websites

nationalgallery.org.uk
john-constable.org.uk
metmuseum.org
nytimes.com
bbc.co.uk/news/entertainment
britishtelephones.com
information-britain.co.uk
princeofwales.gov.uk
hrp.org.uk
telegraph.co.uk
durhamworldheritagesite.com
shropshiretourism.co.uk
hwitbyonline.co.uk
alva.org.uk
hadrianswallcountry.co.uk
pearlykingsandqueens.com/history
seasidehistory.co.uk/seaside
balmoralcastle.com
hrp.org.uk
historicroyalpalaces.com
oxforddnb.com
infoplease.com/country/northern-ireland
history.co.uk/study-topics/history-of-london
postalheritage.org.uk
pearlysociety.co.uk
www.yorkshire-england.co.uk
talktocanada.com
discover-stratford.com
harvardpress.typepad.com
suzanneburdon.com
https://en.wikipedia.org/wiki/Clare_Asquith
guardian.com

Books
Epstein, N., *The Friendly Shakespeare*, 1993
Hughes, A., *The Little Book of Big Words*, 2006
Plowden, A., *Elizabethan England, Life in an Age of Adventure*, 1983
Wiltshire, E.A., *History of the Royal Marsden*, 1998

Index